SUPER SLEUTH

4TH CLASS

Audrey Cooney

g GILL EDUCATION

Gill Education
Hume Avenue
Park West
Dublin 12
www.gilleducation.ie

Gill Education is an imprint of M.H. Gill & Co.

© Audrey Cooney 2017

ISBN: 978-0-7171-71842

Editor: Donna Garvin

Design and layout: Liz White Designs

Illustrations: Derry Dillon

Cover design: Slickfish

Cover illustration: Derry Dillon

For permission to reproduce photographs, the author and publisher gratefully acknowledge the following:
© Alamy: 30, 76; courtesy of European Movement Ireland: 34; © iStock: 29T, 31, 72, 80, 83; courtesy of Kerry County Museum: 29C.

The authors and publisher have made every effort to trace all copyright holders. If, however, any have been inadvertently overlooked, we would be pleased to make the necessary arrangement at the first opportunity.

The paper used in this book is made from the wood pulp of managed forests. For every tree felled, at least one tree is planted, thereby renewing natural resources.

Contents

How to Use this Book

Super Sleuth is a unique mathematical problem-solving series for 1st to 6th Class primary school pupils. Problem-solving requires pupils to understand and explore a problem, find a strategy, use the strategy to solve the problem and look back and reflect on the solution. *Super Sleuth* focuses on the process of problem-solving and the development of the **ten main problem-solving strategies**. The series has **regular built-in revision** units, which consolidate problem-solving skills.

Differentiation ① ② ③

Differentiation is catered for in each unit through the use of **bronze**, **silver** and **gold** medals that indicate the level of difficulty and provide an entry point for every pupil as well as opportunities for **high-achievers** to be challenged.

Collaborative learning

The series facilitates collaborative learning through **whole-class**, **pair** and **group work** activities. This creates an ideal classroom environment for pupils to develop their maths language and thinking, in which the teacher can act as facilitator and every pupil's contribution is valued. Learning can be applied at home through practice.

Opportunity for
pair work

Duties

Reader
Calculator
Checker
Reporter

Opportunity for
group work

Dedicated strategy units

Each book dedicates **five units to a specific strategy** and pupils are encouraged to utilise and apply the strategies where relevant.

Super Sleuth's ten problem-solving strategies:

- Trial and improvement
- Working backwards
- Working systematically
- Logical reasoning
- Visualising/Draw a picture
- Patterns
- Make a table
- Act it out
- Make a model
- Simplify

CLUES

CLUES is a teacher- and pupil-friendly **framework** developed uniquely for *Super Sleuth* to tackle the most common **problem-solving difficulties** experienced in the classroom. It was created in order to promote Bloom's higher forms of thinking in maths education.

Ashley had 17 toffees. She ate 4 after dinner. How many toffees does she have left?

CLUES

Circle the numbers and keywords:
17, 4, toffees, ate

Link with operation needed (+, −, × or ÷):
Ate 4 suggests take away.

Use a strategy: Visualise.

Estimate and calculate:

	H	T	U
My estimate:		1	7
between 10 and 15	−		4
		1	3

Answer: 13

Summarise and check how you got your answer:
I took away 4 toffees from 17 and checked that the answer plus 4 makes 17.

Super Sleuth key features

Weekly structure: Weekly arrangement of work (30 units) and provides four days of work with three to four questions per day.

WALT: Clear learning outcomes are provided at the beginning of each new strand.

Worked example: A worked example using the CLUES framework is provided at the start of new strands to demonstrate a strategy that pupils can follow, allowing them to work independently.

Clear differentiation: Each page is differentiated using bronze, silver and gold medals to show the level of difficulty and give pupils an incentive to progress. The bronze medal indicates a question that the majority of the class should work on independently. The silver medal poses more of a challenge, while the gold medal may require collaborative work in order for the pupils to reach a solution.

Progress recording: Each question and week has a score tracker to help pupils self-assess.

Pair work/group work: Opportunities are provided for pair and group work. Group work can be applied to activities and these specific questions are highlighted throughout the book, where different roles can be assigned to up to four pupils.

Puzzles and challenges: 'Super Sleuth challenge' is an open-ended question based on the maths skills and strand covered in the unit. 'Super Sleuth investigates' is an activity for applying the maths skills/strand of the unit to a situation that could be encountered in real life.

Self-assessment: The self-assessment section for each strand offers pupils an opportunity to reflect on their learning, as well as providing very valuable information to the teacher.

Problem-solving strategies

Trial and improvement

- The strategy of trial and improvement encourages pupils to make a reasonable estimate, giving them a starting point as they attempt to solve the puzzle.
- The pupils are then asked to check their estimate to see if it works as a solution and revise it accordingly.
- By repeating this process and changing their estimate appropriately, pupils should arrive at the correct answer.
- All rough work should be kept as a record of their work.

Example: On a farm there were some hens and cows. Altogether there were 8 heads and 22 feet. How many hens were there?

Working backwards

- Occasionally pupils come across a puzzle in which they are given the final answer and the steps taken to arrive at the answer, but they are not given the data from the start of the puzzle. They must undo each step to get back to the starting point.
- Pupils can draw a diagram to show the known facts and use the inverse operation when working backwards.

Example: Martha removed a loaf of bread from the oven after it had been baking for two hours. If she took it out at 4 o'clock, at what time did she put it into the oven?

Working systematically

- Working systematically requires pupils to work carefully through the information they are given.
- This strategy may incorporate other strategies for pupils to draw upon in order to work out the process of the problem. They might need to make a list, draw a diagram, make a table or explore problems with numerous answers in order to organise and build on the information until they find the solution.

Example: There are six ice-cream flavours to choose from. How many different two-scoop ice-cream cones can be made?

Logical reasoning

- Logical reasoning can be explained as a proper or reasonable way of thinking about something. It requires the pupils to think carefully about the information they have been given and decide on a way of using the information to solve the puzzle.
- Pupils are encouraged to use a step-by-step approach to reach a solution.
- This may involve implementing a strategy such as visualisation or making a table.

Example: Grumpy, Sneezy, Sleepy and Doc are all in line for the cinema. Sleepy is ahead of Grumpy, Sneezy is behind Grumpy and Doc is second. What is their order from first to last?

Visualising / Draw a picture

- Drawing a diagram can help pupils to visualise a puzzle. By doing this, they can make connections within the puzzle and plan how to solve it.
- Diagrams can include tree diagrams, timelines, pictures, symbols and Venn diagrams.

Example: Felix made 12 butterfly buns and iced them. He placed two chocolate buttons on top of each bun. How many chocolate buttons did he use?

Patterns

- This strategy involves pupils investigating how numbers, images or symbols are arranged in a variety of orders.
- Each pattern follows a rule. Pupils may be asked to identify the rule in a pattern, find the missing value(s) or extend the existing pattern. Many things in our world follow a set of rules, so that we know what to expect.

Example: Millie is making a beaded necklace that follows a pattern of red, green, blue. If she uses 18 beads in total, how many red beads will she use?

Make a table

- When puzzles are written in word sentences, they can be confusing for pupils.
- Making a table helps pupils to organise the information that they have and identify the information that they need.

Example: Mikey saves €4 on Monday. Each day after that, he saves twice as much as the day before. How much money will he have saved by Friday?

Act it out

- Acting it out is an effective strategy for pupils who have difficulty visualising a problem.
- Acting out a problem using props such as cubes or string, or in pairs or groups can greatly simplify finding solutions and is an effective strategy for demonstration purposes in front of the whole class.

Example: I have a 5 litre jug and a 3 litre jug. How can I measure out 7 litres of juice using these jugs?

Make a model

- By making a model, the pupils are given an opportunity to showcase their understanding of a specific area of maths. For example, pupils can investigate the properties of 3-D shapes through model building.

Example: Using 26 cocktail sticks and Blu-tack, how many cubes can Emily make and how many cocktail sticks will be left over?

Simplify

There are three ways in which pupils can simplify a puzzle:
- Reword the puzzle using a more familiar setting.
- Break the puzzle down into steps and solve one part at a time.
- Use smaller numbers.

Example: Amy spent $\frac{1}{8}$ of her savings on a new jacket. If she had €320 in savings, how much did the jacket cost?

$\frac{1}{8}$ of €32 = €4 ➡ $\frac{1}{8}$ of €320 = €40

1 Strategy: Logical Reasoning

Day One

When using logical reasoning to solve puzzles, you use a step-by-step approach to reach the solution. This may involve drawing a matrix (a type of grid), making a list or using a diagram to help. You might also make a prediction and test if this was correct.

Try these.

CLUES

1. Áine, Callum, Clodagh and Matthew each hit a golf ball. They reached distances of 205 m, 201 m, 195 m and 212 m. Matthew's distance was less than Callum's. Clodagh's was the farthest distance. The sum of Clodagh and Áine's distances was 407 m. What distance did each child hit their golf ball?

Answers: Áine 212 m, Callum 201 m, Clodagh 212 m, Matthew 205 m   Marks: /4

Adam	Seán	Clodagh	Jamie	Niall
Ellie	Conor	Lien	Keith	Karen

2. One of Clodagh's classmates has won the Spelling Bee, but which one? Use the clues below to identify the winner.
   - The winner is not between two girls with pigtails.
   - The winner is not below a boy on the grid.
   - The winner is not next to a child with a four-letter name.
   - The winner is not the child whose name comes ninth alphabetically.
   - The winner does not have four letters in their name.

Answer: Coner or Niall   Marks: /1

Super Sleuth challenge

Choose one of the children above as the winner of another award and write clues about them. Swap with your partner and solve.

Today's Marks: /5

Day Two Try these.

CL**UE**s

A **matrix** (plural matrices) is a grid with numbers, names or symbols, arranged in rows and columns. We use a matrix and the information that we have to find missing information. Let's try this example:

Three pupils were asked to choose their favourite subject. Each of them chose a different subject. Use the sentences below to work out who has chosen each subject.

	Maths	P.E.	English
Katrina			
Sanjay			
Rachel			

- Katrina said, "I love working out maths puzzles." Place an 'X' in the P.E. and English boxes in Katrina's row and tick the maths box. You also know that Sanjay and Rachel didn't choose maths, because the children chose different subjects. Place an 'X' in their maths boxes.
- Sanjay said, "I love learning about poetry and writing stories." Tick the English box in his row and place an 'X' in the P.E. box. We now know that Rachel didn't choose English. There is only one subject left that Rachel could have chosen. Do you know what it is?
- Rachel said, "I love exercising and playing sports." Were you right?

1 Work out how many pupils attend Sophie's school. The digits in your answer will be 4, 7, 1 and 9.

- 9 is not the first digit, nor is it the third digit.
- 1 is not the second digit, nor is it the last digit.
- 4 is not the last digit.
- 7 is the second digit.
- The number of pupils in Sophie's school is less than 2,000.

	First Digit	Second Digit	Third Digit	Fourth Digit
4				
7				
1				
9				

Answer: [   ]   Marks: [   ] /1

2 Work out who ordered each of the following meals in the café:

- Sophie hates seafood and so does Ethan.
- Abigail ordered the sushi, but Tristan did not order the meatballs.
- Sophie ordered the panini.

	Sushi	Fish Pie	Panini	Meatballs
Sophie				
Tristan				
Ethan				
Abigail				

Marks: [   ] /4

Today's Marks: [   ] /5

Day Three   Try these.

CLUES

1 Kevin, Cathy, Jess and Carl are friends. Can you figure out who is the youngest member of their group using the clues below?

- Cathy is older than Jess, but younger than Carl.
- Carl is younger than Kevin.

Answer: _____   **Marks:** ___ /1

2 Kevin, Cathy, Jess and Carl went shopping for clothes. They spent €15, €16.50, €12 and €9.50. Can you figure out how much they each spent?

- Jess spent €12.
- Kevin spent less than Carl did.
- Cathy spent the biggest sum of money.

Top tip:
Draw a matrix in your copy to help you solve this puzzle.

Answers: Kevin € ___   **Cathy €** ___   **Jess €** ___   **Carl €** ___   **Marks:** ___ /4

3 When Kevin, Cathy, Jess and Carl were queuing in single file to pay for their items, the two girls were standing behind the two boys, Cathy was last in the queue and Kevin was standing directly in front of Jess. Can you figure out their order in the queue from 1st to 4th?

Answers: 1st: ___   **2nd:** ___   **3rd:** ___   **4th:** ___   **Marks:** ___ /4

4 Can you figure out in which position Jess and three of her teammates, Abigail, Pia and Madison, each play on their soccer team?

| captain | goalkeeper | striker | midfielder |

- Abigail prevents the opposition from scoring by protecting the goal.
- Madison is not the captain.
- Pia is not the midfielder.
- Jess's position involves scoring goals, because she is the striker.

Jess	Abigail	Pia	Madison

Marks: ___ /4

Today's Marks: ___ /13

Day Four Try these.

1 When Julius Caesar sent secret messages to his army, he used a code that involved swapping the letters of the alphabet. In the code below, each letter is swapped with the letter that is three places forwards in the alphabet. Complete the code.

A	B	C	D	E	F	G	H	I	J	K	L	M	N	O	P	Q	R	S	T	U	V	W	X	Y	Z
D	E																						A		

Marks: /1

2 Use the completed table above to decipher the following message:

CLIILT	QEB	XOOLTP	LK	QEB	JXM	QL	CFKA	QEB	QOBXPROB

Marks: /1

3 A transposition cipher is created by rearranging the order of the letters in a message into rows or columns. For example, if I wanted to tell someone where the jewels are hidden, I could send them the following cipher: TESIVHWANAEERMSJLEYE. I came up with this by writing the message in a table as shown below. When you read down the columns, starting at the the top left-hand corner, it reads, 'The jewels are in my vase.'

T	E	S	I	V
H	W	A	N	A
E	E	R	M	S
J	L	E	Y	E

Decipher this message: TRLEMIHAESIGEIAADHTNVTNT.

Answer:

Marks: /1

Today's Marks: /3

Total Marks: /26 | I can explain my reasoning clearly. Yes ☐ No ☐

I can use a matrix to solve a puzzle. Yes ☐ No ☐

11

2 Place Value

We are learning to: Read, write and order four-digit numbers. ☐ Round whole numbers to the nearest thousand. ☐ Justify our answers with explanations. ☐

Day One

Puzzle: In what year was I born?

1. The year in which I was born was an odd number.
2. The hundreds digit was 3 times greater than the units digit.
3. The tens digit was 1 greater than the units digit.
4. I was born between 1940 and 1950.

Using the last clue, we can narrow the search to between 1940 and 1950. Using the first clue, we can rule out the even years between 1940 and 1950:

1940	1941	1942	1943	1944	1945	1946	1947	1948	1949	1950

Next, using the second clue, we look for years in which the hundreds digit is 3 times greater than the units digit and rule out the others:

1940	1941	1942	1943	1944	1945	1946	1947	1948	1949	1950

This leaves 1943 and the third clue confirms that this is the correct answer.

> Create your own place value puzzles in the same style as this example.

Try these.

1,263	1,498	3,175	4,883	3,900	4,806

1 Place the numbers above in order, starting with the **largest**.

Marks: ☐ /1

2 Round each of the numbers above to the nearest thousand.

Marks: ☐ /1

3 Which number is closer to 4,000: 3,175 or 4,883? Explain your answer to a partner. 🗨

Answer: _____   Marks: ☐ /1

Strand: Number **Strand Unit:** Place Value

Today's Marks: ☐ /3

Day Two   Try these.

You are the teacher today! Correct Anthony's homework.
If you find a mistake, write the correct answer and explain
what he did wrong.

1. Anthony was asked to put eight numbers in the correct
   order, starting with the smallest.

3,069	3,096	3,306	3,369	3,396	3,663	3,636	3,696

Is his answer correct? Explain.

Marks: /1

2. For patterns homework, he was asked to continue a sequence.

1,185, 1,110, 1,035, <u>950, 875, 800</u>

Is his answer correct? Explain.

Marks: /1

3. A mystery number rounded up to the nearest
   thousand is 4,000. Anthony was asked to think
   of the smallest number that this could be.

> I think the smallest number this could be is 3,501, because any number greater than 3,500 will round up to 4,000.

Is his answer correct? Explain.

Marks: /1

Super Sleuth investigates

Which one of the children do you agree
with, Ciarán or Rachel? Give reasons for
your answer.

> No, that's not right. We need the number zero. We use it every day.

> The number zero is useless. That's why it's called nothing!

Day Three Try these.

CLUES

1. Write 5 different decimal numbers to two decimal places, e.g. 24.54. There are two rules: your tens digit must be 4 and your tenths ($\frac{1}{10}$) digit must be 5. Show your numbers on the abacuses.

| T | U | $\frac{1}{10}$ | $\frac{1}{100}$ | | T | U | $\frac{1}{10}$ | $\frac{1}{100}$ | | T | U | $\frac{1}{10}$ | $\frac{1}{100}$ | | T | U | $\frac{1}{10}$ | $\frac{1}{100}$ | | T | U | $\frac{1}{10}$ | $\frac{1}{100}$ |

Marks: /5

2. Write the numbers above in order, starting with the smallest.

Marks: /1

3. Add 1.05 to each of the numbers above.

Marks: /5

4. Ciarán thinks that 1.34 is greater than 1.4. Rachel thinks that 1.4 is greater than 1.34. What do you think? Draw a picture to prove your answer.

But 1.34 is a longer number than 1.4!

Marks: /1

Super Sleuth challenge

How many four-digit numbers can you make using the digits 5, 8, 7 and 1? There are two rules: the digit 8 must not go in the thousands place and the digit 7 must not go in the tens place.

Today's Marks: /12

Day Four Try these.

Use your copy to work out the answers to these puzzles. Choose a number from 1 to 9,999 and use it to complete the following:

(1) My number is [　　　]   Is it odd or even? [　　　]

Half of my number is [　　　]   Double my number is [　　　]

Thousands	Hundreds	Tens	Units

Marks: [　] /1

(2) [　] divides evenly into my number.   My number multiplied by 5 is [　　]

Word form: [　　　　　　　　　　]

Expanded form: [　　　　　　　　　]

Marks: [　] /2

(3) This is my number rounded ...

To the nearest 10:	To the nearest 100:	To the nearest 1,000:

If I had this amount of money, I could buy [　　　　　]

Marks: [　] /3

Today's Marks: [　] /6

Super Sleuth challenge

Use a stopwatch or the classroom clock to time how long it takes each player to complete their task in each round.

Round	Player A	Player B
1	Count in 2s up to 24.	Count in 3s up to 36.
2	Count in 200s up to 1400.	Count in 10s up to 70.
3	Count in 0.1s up to 1 whole unit.	Count in 0.2s up to 2.0.
4	Count in 0.25s up to 1.5.	Count in 0.5s up to 3.0.

Total Marks: [　] /24   Was it easy being the teacher on Day Two?   Yes [　] No [　]

Explain your answer. [　　　　　　]

Was there any part of this unit that you found difficult? [　　　　　　]

15

3 Addition and Subtraction

We are learning to: Add and subtract four-digit numbers. ☐
Solve word problems involving addition and subtraction. ☐

Day One

CLUEs

Helen went to the mart and saw the following animals:

Kevin	Frank	Mary	Patricia	Mike	Nora
915 kg	1,027 kg	585 kg	610 kg	54 kg	57 kg
€1,720	€1,865	€1,256	€1,378	€114	€121

1 How much would Frank, Mary and Patricia cost altogether?

Write your estimate for each question before doing your calculations.

Estimate: _____ Answer: _____ Marks: ___ /1

2 Helen is thinking of buying Kevin and Mary or Patricia and Frank.
(a) If she wants to buy the heavier pair of animals, which option should she choose? **(b)** How much heavier is this option than the other pair of animals?

Answers: (a) _____ (b) _____ Marks: ___ /2

3 Helen decides to buy one bull, one cow and the two lambs. The maximum weight that her trailer can carry is 1,600 kg. Is it possible for her to bring home the four animals today? Explain your answer.

Answer: _____ Marks: ___ /1

Strand: Number **Strand Unit:** Operations – addition and subtraction

Today's Marks: ___ /4

Day Two Try these.

1. Helen had 2,645 bales of hay stored in her shed, 579 bales in the field next to her house and 356 bales in the field next to the river. How many bales did she have altogether? Estimate first.

Write your estimate for each question before doing your calculations.

Estimate: Answer: Marks: /1

2. Helen sold 1,475 of her bales of hay. How many bales did she have left?

Estimate: Answer: Marks: /1

3. After selling her hay, Helen got a delivery of 3 loads of turf. In the first load, there were 1,943 sods. In the second load, there were 2,108. If the total number of sods delivered was 6,254, how many were in the third load?

Estimate: Answer: Marks: /1

4. Helen's neighbour Brendan has 3,039 more sods of turf than Helen and double the amount of bales of hay that she had left after she sold some in question 2 above. How many (a) sods and (b) bales does Brendan have?

Answers: (a)   (b)   Marks: /2

Today's Marks: /5   **17**

Day Three Try these.

CLUES

1. The table shows how much milk four cows produce per week. How many litres of milk do all four cows produce in one week?

Daisy	Bessy	Lulu	Maggie
151 l	145 l	177 l	124 l

Answer: _____ Marks: ___ /1

2. What is the difference in litres between the amount of milk provided by Maggie and Lulu in four weeks?

Top tip: Use patterns and work systematically.

Answer: _____ Marks: ___ /1

3. Charlie worked a different number of hours every week, but his pay followed a pattern. Use the grid below to figure out what that pattern was and work out what Charlie was paid in **(a)** June and **(b)** July. Fill in the table.

January	February	March	April	May	June	July
€250	€400	€700	€1,150	€1,750		

Marks: ___ /2

4. If this pattern continues for the rest of the year, what will be the first month in which Charlie earns more money than he earned in May, June and July combined?

Top tip: Draw a table to record Charlie's earnings from July onwards.

Answer: _____ Marks: ___ /1

Today's Marks: ___ /5

Day Four Try these.

CLUES

1. Using the digits 4, 9, 3 and 8, make as many four-digit numbers as you can that are:

(a) Less than 5,000		(b) Greater than 5,000	

Marks: /2

2. Using your four-digit numbers above: **(a)** Find the difference between the largest number and smallest number. **(b)** Add the two smallest numbers that are less than 5,000 together.

Answers: (a)   (b)   Marks: /2

Today's Marks: /4

Super Sleuth challenge

The total number of animal legs on Helen's farm was 382. How many animals do you think there were?

Super Sleuth investigates

a	b	c	d	e	f	g	h	i	j	k	l	m
26	25	24	23	22	21	20	19	18	17	16	15	14
n	o	p	q	r	s	t	u	v	w	x	y	z
13	12	11	10	9	8	7	6	5	4	3	2	1

Duties

Reader
Calculator
Checker
Reporter

Using the grid above, can you find words that match the values in the table below? Plan with your group how you will solve this puzzle.

	Girl's name	Boy's name	City	Country	Fruit
Less than 60					
61–100					
101–160					

Total Marks: /18 | My favourite activity in this unit was

I would like to improve

4 Multiplication

We are learning to: Identify relevant information in puzzles. ☐ Solve multiplication puzzles. ☐

Day One — Study the steps used to solve the problem in the example below.

Siobhán bought 7 books costing €9.50 each and 5 copies costing 85c each. How much did she spend on books?

CLUES

Circle the numbers and keywords:
   7 books, €9.50 each, spend on books (Ignore the copies.)

Link with operation needed (+, −, × or ÷): Multiply (×).

Use a strategy: Simplify.

Estimate and calculate:
   My estimate: 7 × €10 = €70, so less than €70

$$\begin{array}{r} €\ \ 9.50 \\ \times\ \ \ \ \ \ 7 \\ \hline €66.50 \end{array}$$

Answer: €66.50

Summarise and check how you got your answer:
   I realised that I did not need the information about the copies. I multiplied 7 times €9.50.

Top tip: We must identify the information that we need to answer the question. Information that we don't need is called surplus data. Find the surplus data in the questions below.

Try these.

CLUES

1. For her wedding, Steph ordered 6 bouquets of flowers costing €45 each and 4 rolls of ribbon costing €5.75 each. How much did she spend on flowers?

   Answer: _____ Marks: ___ /1

2. Steph's best friend created a beautiful booklet for her wedding and printed over 145 copies. Each page had 235 words. If there were 26 pages in the booklet, how many words were in one booklet?

   Answer: _____ Marks: ___ /1

3. Steph and her husband went on a 7-night cruise for their honeymoon costing €1,200 each. If the cruise ship had 19 decks, with 185 guests and 2 swimming pools on each deck, how many guests were on the ship?

   Answer: _____ Marks: ___ /1

Today's Marks: ___ /3

Day Two Try these.

1 A gardener earns €115 per day. If she works for 12 days at Elmview National School, how much will she earn altogether?

Answer: Marks: /1

2 The principal of Elmview National School went to a garden centre to buy some equipment for the school. A trowel costs €6.50 and a pair of gloves costs €7.50. If each of the 216 pupils needs a trowel and a pair of gloves, how much will these items cost altogether?

Answer: Marks: /1

3 At the garden centre, a raised flower bed costs €7.75 and a trellis costs €10.25. If the principal decides to buy 32 of each plus a shed costing €965.50, how much will she spend on these items altogether?

Answer: Marks: /1

4 If the principal has a budget of €5,950, does she have enough money to pay the gardener and buy all of the items above?

☐ Yes, she has enough money, with €   to spare.

☐ No, she does not have enough money. She needs an extra €   . Marks: /1

Day Three — Try these.

Top tip:

You can round the numbers in a puzzle to help you estimate, e.g. 58 × 2 = ___

Firstly, round 58 to the nearest 10.

60 × 2 = 120

120 is your estimate.

Study this grid. The answers have been filled in. Can you work out how the answers were calculated? Once you have worked it out, fill in the missing numbers in the grids below. Use your copy for extra rough work.

7	2	14
1	5	5
7	10	70

1

24	12	
7	3	

Marks: ☐ /1

2

58	2	
8	9	

Marks: ☐ /1

3

	2	96
5		35
240	14	

Marks: ☐ /1

4

2		36
28	9	
	162	

Marks: ☐ /1

Puzzle power ✏️

Each emoticon represents a different number less than 5. These numbers were multiplied to reach the answers in the fourth row and the fourth column. Can you work out the value of each emoticon and fill in the rest of the answers?

😍	😂	😆	
😂	😎	😎	
😍	😍	😍	64
32		8	

Today's Marks: ☐ /4

Day Four — Try these.

Dice Multiplication

In a group of four, take turns rolling a die to decide what your multiplication questions will be. Each player will roll the die 5 times in order to choose the numbers for one question. For example, the first player may roll the numbers shown.

1st roll	2	
2nd roll	6	
3rd roll	4	
4th roll	4	
5th roll	3	

Those numbers are then placed in the grid as follows:

	H	T	U
	2	6	4
×		4	3
+			0

Once you have all of your numbers, work out the answers. Compare your workings within the group. Use a calculator to check your work.

1

	H	T	U
×			
+			0

Marks: /1

2

	H	T	U
×			
+			0

Marks: /1

3

	H	T	U
×			
+			0

Marks: /1

4

	H	T	U
×			
+			0

Marks: /1

Today's Marks: /4

Puzzle power

When I multiply three numbers by one another, the answer is 48. What might those three numbers be? Might one of your numbers be 0? Why/Why not?

Total Marks: /15 | Surplus data means _____

I round the numbers in my maths, because _____

5 🐕 Length

Day One Study the steps used to solve the problem in the example below.

A scalene triangle has a perimeter of $15\frac{1}{4}$ m. If one side of the triangle is 4.8 m and another is $5\frac{7}{10}$ m, what is the length of the third side?

CLUE**s**

Circle the numbers and keywords:
perimeter of $15\frac{1}{4}$ m, 4.8 m, $5\frac{7}{10}$ m, third side?

Link with operation needed (+, −, × or ÷):
Add (+) and subtract (−).

Use a strategy: Simplify by changing the values to decimals.

Estimate and calculate:
My estimate: 4 m

$$\begin{array}{r} 4.8 \text{ m} \\ + 5.7 \text{ m} \\ \hline 10.5 \text{ m} \end{array}$$

$$\begin{array}{r} 15.25 \text{ m} \\ - 10.5 \text{ m} \\ \hline 4.75 \text{ m} \end{array}$$

Answer: 4.75 m

Summarise and check how you got your answer:
I changed the values to decimal form. I added the length of the two sides and subtracted this from the perimeter.

Top tip: Round the values when estimating:
15. 25 m ➜ 15 m
4.8 m ➜ 5 m
5.7 m ➜ 6 m
5 m + 6 m = 11 m
15 m − 11 m = 4 m

Try these.

CLUE**s**

1. The lengths in the table are given in decimal and fraction form. Can you change them to m and cm?

Marks: ☐ /5

	Length	Length in m and cm
Couch	1.75 m	
Dining room table	$2\frac{9}{10}$ m	
Window	2.05 m	
Television	0.5 m	
Fireplace	$1\frac{1}{4}$ m	

2. If a room has 3 windows of the length shown in the table above, what is the total length of the windows in the room? Write your answer in cm.

Answer: _____ Marks: ☐ /1

Today's Marks: ☐ /6

Day Two Try these.

1 The perimeter of an equilateral triangle is 468 cm. What is the length of one of its sides? Write your answer in metres using a decimal point.

Top tip: An equilateral triangle has three sides of equal length.

Answer: _____ Marks: ___ /1

2 What is the perimeter of the football pitch?

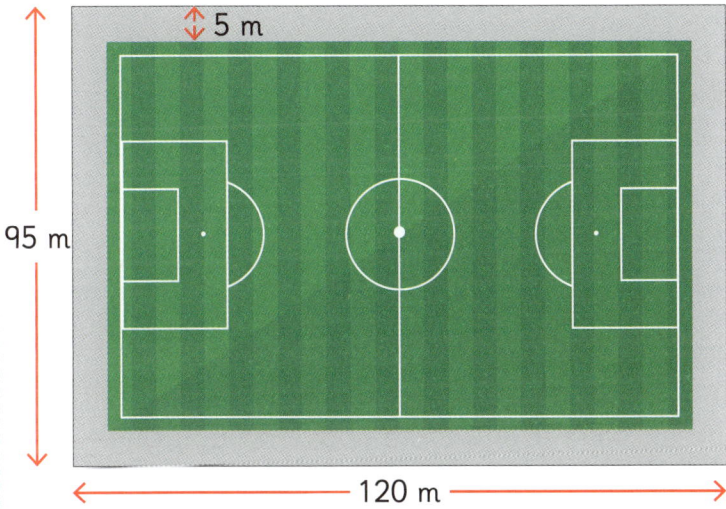

Top tip: To find the perimeter of a 2-D shape, add up all of its sides.

5 m

95 m

120 m

Answer: _____ Marks: ___ /1

3 Which of these shapes has the greatest perimeter: **(a)** a regular octagon with sides measuring 5.95 cm or **(b)** a regular pentagon with sides measuring 8.75 cm?

Answer: _____ Marks: ___ /1

4 A square has a perimeter of 56.4 m. If this square was combined with three others to create one large square, what would the new perimeter be?

Answer: _____ Marks: ___ /1

Day Three Try these.

The Monaco Grand Prix is a Formula 1 race that takes place on the streets of Monaco. The distances in the grid below are linked to facts about the Monaco Grand Prix. Answer the questions and write the relevant facts in the table.

Clues

20 km	
260.52 km	
33 km	
155.55 km	

1. The Monaco track has three lengths of safety railings measuring 7.25 km, $15\frac{6}{10}$ km and 10 km 150 m. What is the total length of the railings?

Answer: Marks: /1

2. One lap of the Monaco Grand Prix track measures over 3 km, but less than 4 km. The race is 78 laps long. Which of the answers in the table above do you think is the total distance of the race?

Answer: Marks: /1

3. François travelled from Nice to Monaco for the Grand Prix. He drove at an average speed of 100 km per hour and reached Monaco in just 12 minutes. How far is Nice from Monaco?

Answer: Marks: /1

4. Fernando Alonso can drive almost 120 km in 45 minutes in his race car. How many kilometres can he travel in one hour?

Answer: Marks: /1

Today's Marks: /4

Day Four Try these.

1 Estimate and then measure the perimeter of each of the items or areas in your school listed below. Write the measuring instrument that you used. Use the blank rows to record the perimeter of two items of your choice.

Item/area	Estimate	Perimeter	Instrument Used
Super Sleuth book			
Desk			
Classroom door			
Classroom			
Yard			

Marks: ☐ /1

2 Write your name across this grid, leaving a 1 cm square between each letter. Before you do so, estimate what you think the total perimeter of the letters in your name will be.

Estimate: ☐ Answer: ☐ Marks: ☐ /1

3 Which of your classmates do you think has the name with **(a)** the shortest perimeter and **(b)** the longest perimeter? Discuss your predictions with your classmates. Were they correct?

Answers: (a) ☐ (b) ☐

Today's Marks: ☐ /2

Total Marks: ☐ /16 | I can rename units of length using decimal or fraction form. Yes ☐ No ☐

I can explain how to find the perimeter of a 2-D shape. Yes ☐ No ☐

6 Revision 1

The Wild Atlantic Way

NORTHERN HEADLANDS

SURF COAST

BAY COAST

CLIFF COAST

SOUTHERN PENINSULAS

HAVEN COAST

Sorcha and her family are travelling along the Wild Atlantic Way, a scenic 2,500 km stretch of Ireland's coastline. Solve these puzzles about the trip.

Day One Try these.

CLUEs

1. When the tide is low at Malin Head, the wreck of a ship named the *Twilight* can be seen. Work out what year the *Twilight* sank.

   - The *Twilight* sank between 1880 and 1890.
   - The hundreds and tens digits are the same.
   - When you add the digits of this year together, the sum is 26.
   - When you add the thousands and hundreds digits, the answer is the same as the digit in the units place.
   - The units digit minus the thousands digit will give you the digits in the hundreds and tens places.

   Answer: _____ Marks: ___ /1

2. In the 20th century, John Alcock and Arthur Brown made the first non-stop transatlantic flight from Newfoundland in Canada to Clifden, Co. Galway, where they crash-landed safely in Derrigimlagh Bog. Work out the year in which this happened.

   - This event took place between 1910 and 1920.
   - The thousands and hundreds digits add up to ten.
   - The tens and units digits add up to ten.
   - The digit in the thousands place is the same as the digit in the tens place.
   - The digit in the hundreds place is the same as the digit in the units place.

   Answer: _____ Marks: ___ /1

3. **(a)** Round the years from questions 1 and 2 above to the nearest ten and hundred.
   (b) Which of these years is closest to 1905?

	Nearest 10	Nearest 100
The year the *Twilight* sank:		
The year Alcock and Brown crash-landed:		

   Answer: _____ Marks: ___ /5

Strand: Number **Strand Units:** Place Value; Operations – addition, subtraction and multiplication
Strand: Measures **Strand Unit:** Length

Today's Marks: ___ /7

Day Two Try these.

1 Sorcha's family drove past Ireland's second highest mountain, Mount Brandon, while they were in Kerry. If Ireland's highest mountain, Carrauntoohil is 85 m higher than Mount Brandon and Carrauntoohil is 1,038 m high, how high is Mount Brandon?

Answer: _____ Marks: ____ /1

2 The Kerry County Museum and Medieval Experience has recreated the streets of Tralee as they looked in the year 1450. How many years ago was this?

Answer: _____ Marks: ____ /1

3 Sorcha's family attended a funfair in Tralee and spent time playing arcade games. Sorcha scored 2,376 points. Mum scored 125 more points than Sorcha. Dad scored 54 more points than Mum. Conor scored 239 more points than Dad. How many points did Conor score?

Answer: _____ Marks: ____ /1

4 If Mum and Dad combined their scores and Sorcha and Conor combined their scores, which pair would win and by how much?

Answer: _____ Marks: ____ /2

Super Sleuth investigates

Ask permission from your teacher or a parent to use Google Maps to plan a route along the Wild Atlantic Way. What destinations would you visit? How many kilometres of the route would you travel? Write three questions you could ask a friend about the route.

Today's Marks: ____ /5

Day Three Try these.

CLUES

Super Sleuth challenge

One of the questions below includes surplus data. When you find out which question it is, fill in the following:

I found surplus data in question [ ]. The surplus data that I found was

[   ]

1 The Clifden Arts Festival is held annually. There are 13 rows in the Clifden Station House Theatre, with 15 seats in each row. How many seats are there altogether?

Answer: [   ] Marks: [   ] /1

2 When the magician Magnifico came to the Clifden Station House Theatre, all of the tickets sold out. If a ticket cost €18, how much money did the theatre make that night?

Answer: [   ] Marks: [   ] /1

3 Magnifico's show was 2 hours long, with an interval 50 minutes into the show. Popcorn and jellies were sold at this time. The popcorn cost 95c and 32 packets were sold. The jellies cost 75c and 88 packets were sold. How much money was spent on popcorn and jellies altogether?

Answer: [   ] Marks: [   ] /1

4 The seats at the Clifden Station House Theatre are due to be repaired. 104 of them will cost €12 each for repairs. The rest will cost €19 each for repairs. How much will it cost to repair all of the seats? Use your copy to work it out.

Answer: [   ] Marks: [   ] /1

Today's Marks: [   ] /4

Day Four Try these.

1 Sorcha and her family jumped in the air while posing for a funny photograph of Benbulben. Match each person to the height that they jumped using the following clues:

- Mum's jump was the lowest.
- Sorcha's jump was 0.55 m less than 1 m.
- Conor jumped over $\frac{1}{2}$ m, but his jump wasn't the highest.
- Dad's jump was greater than Mum and Sorcha's jumps added together.

Benbulben

0.65 m	0.74 m	0.27 m	0.45 m

Marks: /1

2 Sorcha's family cycled 195 km of the Beara Way over a few days. On day one, they cycled 35 km. Every second day, they alternated between cycling 35 km or 30 km. How many days did it take them to complete the journey? Make a table in your copy to help you solve this puzzle.

Answer: ____ Marks: /1

3 The combined height above sea level of **(a)** Dursey Island's cable car and **(b)** the highest point of the Cliffs of Moher is 464 m. The difference between their heights is 36 m and the cable car is the higher of the two. Can you work out the height of each?

Cable car

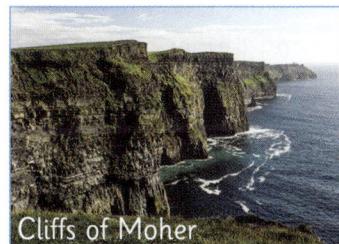

Cliffs of Moher

Top tip:
Each of your two answers will be between 210 m and 255 m and both answers are even numbers.

Answers: (a) ____ (b) ____ Marks: /2

Today's Marks: /4

Super Sleuth investigates

Sorcha's birthday cake is 12 cm long. If it takes 6 seconds to cut one slice, how many seconds will it take to cut 4 slices that are 3 cm wide? Draw a diagram to help you.

Total Marks: /20   31

7 Strategy: Make a Table

Day One

Making a table is a strategy that helps you to organise the information in a maths story and identify the information that you need.

Try these.

1 Donna and Emma are saving for their holiday. Donna started with €25 and is saving €7.50 per week. Emma started with €40 and is saving €5 per week.

(a) Estimate who will have saved the most after 7 weeks.

(b) Complete the table with Donna and Emma's savings.

	Start	Week 1	Week 2	Week 3	Week 4	Week 5	Week 6	Week 7
Donna	€25							
Emma	€40							

Top tip:
Always plan your table before you begin. Use a pencil and a ruler to draw your table.

Marks: /1

2 After how many weeks will Donna and Emma have the same amount of money saved?

Answer: Marks: /1

3 If both girls are aiming to save €100, how many weeks will it take each girl to reach her target? Make a table to help you solve this number story.

Answers: Donna Emma Marks: /1

Today's Marks: /3

Day Two Try these.

1 Daisy decided to reduce the amount of sweets that she eats. She used to eat a packet of 38 per day. On day one, she ate only 34 and on day two, she ate only 30. If this pattern continued, how many days did it take to reach her target of just 2 sweets per day?

Answer: ___ Marks: __ /1

2 Rocco has an equal number of €1 coins and 50c coins. If he has €13.50 in total, how many of each coin does he have?

Answer: ___ Marks: __ /1

3 Wonder Kidz organises children's birthday parties. It charges €110 for the first five children and €30 for each additional child. If Evie's parents have a budget of €200 to spend on her birthday party, how many guests can Evie invite? (Be careful! Remember that Evie is included in the cost of the party.)

Answer: ___ Marks: __ /1

4 How many hours will it take a red car travelling at 75 km per hour to overtake a blue car travelling at 55 km per hour if the blue car started two hours before the red car?

Answer: ___ Marks: __ /1

Remember to make a table to help you solve each number story.

Today's Marks: __ /4

33

Day Three Try these.

1 If a book is 1 hour late back to the library, the fine is 15c. For each hour after that, the fine is doubled. If Josh's library book is 6 hours late, will he be able to pay his fine with just two €2 coins? Use the table to work out the answer.

Hours late	1	2	3	4		
Fine	15c	30c	60c	€1.20		

Answer: _____ Marks: ___ /1

2 The 1st prize in a raffle was double the amount of the 2nd prize. The 2nd prize was three times bigger than the 3rd prize. The 4th prize was $\frac{1}{4}$ the amount of the 3rd prize. If the 3rd prize was €40, **(a)** how much was the 1st prize and **(b)** what was the total amount of prize money?

Answers: (a) _____ (b) _____ Marks: ___ /1

3 Josh's class are taking part in the Blue Star Programme. On Europe Day, they will conduct a Handshake for Europe. If there are 15 children in Josh's maths class, and each child shakes hands once with the rest of their classmates, how many handshakes will there be altogether? Find the pattern and record the results in the table below.

Blue Star
Programme

Top tip:
Act it out.

Children	1	2	3	4	5	6	7	8	9	10	11	12	13	14	15
Handshakes	0	1	3	6	10										

Marks: ___ /1

4 Josh is the first runner on a relay team of four athletes. Each runner must run 65 m farther than the previous runner. If the final runner runs 405 m, what is the combined distance that the team runs? You could make a table and work backwards to work out the answer.

Answer: _____ Marks: ___ /1

Today's Marks: ___ /4

Day Four Try these.

1 Mr Farrell came to school with a birthday badge on his jumper. Sam asked, "How old are you, Teacher?"

Mr Farrell replied, "If you can solve this puzzle, you will know how old I am! 6 years from now, my age will be three times greater than yours will be."

If Sam is 9 years old, what age is Mr Farrell?

Answer: _____ **Marks:** /1

2 After Sam had worked out Mr Farrell's age, he told his friend, "Mr Farrell will be half my grandad's age in a few years' time. My grandad is 84 years old now." Make a table to find out how old Sam's grandad will be when Mr Farrell is half his age.

Answer: _____ **Marks:** /1

3 All of the children in Sam's school sang 'Happy Birthday' to Mr Farrell. If there are 121 pupils in Sam's school and 5 out of every 11 are boys, how many girls are there? Continue the table below to work out the answer.

Boys	5										
Girls											
Total	11										

Answer: _____ **Marks:** /1

Today's Marks: /3

Super Sleuth challenge

Invent a number story to match the table below. In your copy, write two questions based on your number story and share them with your partner.

	Month 1	Month 2	Month 3	Month 4	Month 5
	€100	€250	€550	€1,150	€2,350

Total Marks: ____ /14 | I can use a table to solve maths stories. **Yes** ☐ **No** ☐

I like / dislike using tables, because _____

35

8 Division

We are learning to: Divide a three-digit number by a one-digit number. ☐
Work systematically to solve division puzzles. ☐

Day One Study the steps used to solve the problem in the example below.

One page of *The Emerald Times* has 5 columns with a total of 995 words. How many words would you find in one column if the words are shared equally between the columns?

CLUES

Circle the numbers and keywords: 5 columns, 995 words

Link with operation needed (+, −, × or ÷): Divide (÷).

Use a strategy: Logical reasoning

Estimate and calculate:

| Round 995 to the nearest 10: 1,000 ÷ 5 = 200 | 995 ÷ 5 = 199 | **Answer:** 199 |

Summarise and check how you got your answer:
The words were shared equally between the columns, so I divided 995 by 5.

> You will need a newspaper for an activity on day three. Keep an eye out for one!

Try these.

CLUES

1. Aidan is in charge of the sports department at *The Emerald Times*. He accepted an award of €945 to be shared equally between himself and 6 other journalists in his department. How much did they each receive?

   Answer: _____ Marks: ___ /1

2. Aidan has 4 hours and 27 minutes to write three articles. If he divides his time equally between the three, how long will it take him to write each article? Change the time to minutes before you start.

   Answer: _____ Marks: ___ /1

3. At *The Emerald Times*, the sports, news and business departments are located on the same floor. There are three times more business journalists than sports journalists. News has twice as many journalists as business. The floor is divided into 10 offices with an equal number of journalists in each. How many are there in each office?

   Answer: _____ Marks: ___ /1

Today's Marks: ___ /3

Day Two Try these.

Clues

1 Many homes in Glencar Woods get their newspaper delivered every day. Altogether, they spend €795 per day on newspapers. If each newspaper costs €3, how many homes have theirs delivered?

Answer: _____ **Marks:** ___ /1

2 If Scribbles Newsagents sold 532 copies of *The Emerald Times* over 7 days and 375 copies of *The Munster Herald* over 5 days, which paper sold more copies per day and by how many?

Answer: _____ **Marks:** ___ /2

3 **(a)** Use the clues below to work out the number of pages that there are in 7 copies of *The Emerald Times*. Work systematically to eliminate numbers from the grid and you will be left with the answer.

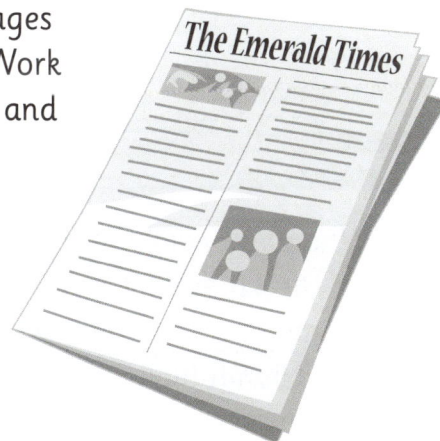

The Emerald Times

Top tip: Working systematically means completing a series of tasks in order to reach the solution.

- Eliminate all of the numbers that 2 cannot divide evenly into.
- Eliminate all of the numbers that 5 divides evenly into.
- Eliminate all of the numbers that 8 cannot divide evenly into.
- You should have two numbers left. The answer is the number that 7 divides evenly into.

23	248	123	47	206	124	87	224
175	59	133	140	126	250	279	236
147	265	278	212	245	198	306	200

(b) Work out the number of pages that there are in 1 copy of *The Emerald Times*.

Answers: (a) _____ **(b)** _____ **Marks:** ___ /2

Day Three Try these.

1 Olivia has been asked to organise a party to celebrate a special anniversary for *The Emerald Times*. Use the following clues to find out how old the newspaper is:

- The newspaper is between 70 and 80 years old.
- It is not possible to divide 2 evenly into this number.
- The number 3 divides evenly into this number.

Answer: _____ Marks: ___ /1

2 Niamh is making up goody bags for everyone who attends the party. Each bag must contain 6 chocolates. If there are 755 chocolates, how many goody bags can be filled and how many chocolates will be left over?

Answer: _____ Marks: ___ /1

3 When you combine the number of years that Aidan, Olivia and Niamh have worked at *The Emerald Times*, the total is 26. Olivia has worked there 4 times as long as Niamh, but only half as long as Aidan. Work out for how many years Aidan, Olivia and Niamh have worked for the newspaper. Use trial and improvement to solve this number story.

Answers: Aidan: _____ Olivia: _____ Niamh: _____ Marks: ___ /3

Super Sleuth investigates

Find as many examples of maths in your newspaper as possible. Cut out 5 examples and present them to your classmates. Can you think of 3 division questions that you could ask about your newspaper?

Today's Marks: ___ /5

Day Four — Try these.

In Unit 4, dealing with multiplication, you solved puzzles like questions 1 and 2 below. Use your division and multiplication skills to find the missing values.

CLUES

1

	5	
9	108	
81	60	

Marks: ☐ /1

2

	8	
		9
36	24	864

Marks: ☐ /1

3 *The Emerald Times* hosts an annual golf competition. If four people fit in one golf cart and there are 98 contestants, how many golf carts are needed?

Answer: _____   Marks: ☐ /1

4 Newspapers often include brainteasers. Can you solve each of the following brainteasers in 30 seconds?

15 × 2	÷ 3	× 9	+ 10	÷ 4	÷ 5	times itself	÷ 25

108 ÷ 12	× 4	÷ 3	× 5	÷ 10	+ 64	÷ 7	÷ 5

Marks: ☐ /2

Today's Marks: ☐ /5

Puzzle power ✏️

In a group of four, each person must choose different numbers to complete the number sentence below and then write a number story to match it.

36 ÷ ☐ = ☐

Total Marks: ☐ /18 | When I hear the word 'division', these words pop into my head:

_____

I can divide a three-digit number by a one-digit number without and with remainders. Yes ☐ No ☐

9 Fractions

We are learning to: Compare and order fractions on a number line. ☐
Use maths language when discussing fractions. ☐

Day One Study the steps used to solve the problem in the example below.

Lily is $\frac{1}{3}$ of her aunt Rachel's age. If Rachel is 33, how old is Lily?

CLUEs

Circle the numbers and keywords: $\frac{1}{3}$, 33, how old?

Link with operation needed (+, −, × or ÷): Divide (÷).

Use a strategy: Visualise.

33

Estimate and calculate:

My estimate: $\frac{1}{3}$ means to divide by 3

$33 ÷ 3 = 11$

Answer: 11 years old

Summarise and check how you got your answer:
11 × 3 is 33, which is Rachel's age, so my answer is correct.

Try these.

CLUEs

1. Lily invited 7 of her friends to her birthday party at a roller disco. $\frac{1}{4}$ of the group, including Lily, wore white roller skates. The remaining children wore black roller skates. How many children wore black roller skates?

Answer: _____ Marks: ___ /1

2. There were 4 other children at the roller disco at the same time as Lily and her friends. $\frac{1}{3}$ of all of the children there wore knee pads, $\frac{1}{6}$ wore elbow pads and the rest wore no protective clothing. How many children did not wear protective clothing?

Answer: _____ Marks: ___ /1

3. When 50 minutes of the roller disco had passed, Lily and her friends were $\frac{2}{3}$ of the way through the party. How much time did they have in total at the roller disco? Write your answer in hours and minutes.

Answer: _____ Marks: ___ /1

Today's Marks: ___ /3

Day Two   Try these.

1 Lily and 9 of her friends entered a race called 'Stuck in the Mud'. Together, they made up $\frac{1}{12}$ of the entire number of contestants in the race. How many contestants took part in the race altogether?

Answer: _____   **Marks:** [ ] /1

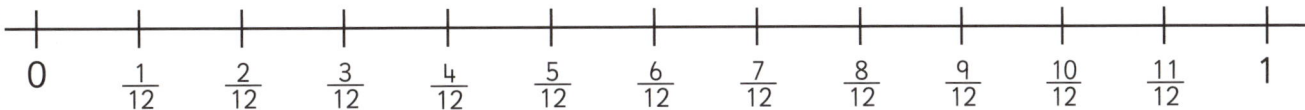

2 3 of Lily's 9 friends did not enjoy the race. What fraction of her friends did not enjoy the race?

Answer: _____   **Marks:** [ ] /1

3 During the race, the children had lower obstacles to climb than the adults. The adults' Wonky Wall was 171 cm high. The children's Wonky Wall was $\frac{7}{9}$ of 171 cm. How high was the children's Wonky Wall?

Answer: _____   **Marks:** [ ] /1

4 The table below shows the distance of the racecourse that Lily and each of her friends had completed after 30 minutes. Put their positions in order on the number line, starting with the child who had completed the shortest distance.

Top tip: Use a fraction wall to help you convert the fractions in question 4 to members of the twelfths family.

Lily	Carl	Josh	Mira	Ben	Matt	Oran	Lucy	Dee	Sile
$\frac{1}{2}$	$\frac{11}{12}$	$\frac{3}{4}$	$\frac{5}{6}$	$\frac{1}{4}$	$\frac{2}{3}$	$\frac{7}{12}$	$\frac{1}{3}$	$\frac{1}{6}$	$\frac{5}{12}$

Marks: [ ] /10

```
|      |      |      |      |      |      |      |      |      |      |      |      |
0    1/12   2/12   3/12   4/12   5/12   6/12   7/12   8/12   9/12  10/12  11/12   1
```

Day Three Try these.

Clues

1 Lily's gran gave her €15 for her birthday. Lily spent $\frac{1}{3}$ of this money buying a new pencil case and colours. How much did she have left?

Answer: _____ Marks: [ ] /1

2 Lily used the rest of the money that her gran gave her to buy a cinema ticket and popcorn. She spent $\frac{4}{5}$ of the money on the ticket. How much did the popcorn cost?

Answer: _____ Marks: [ ] /1

3 $\frac{5}{12}$ of the people at the cinema were girls. If there were 25 girls, how many people were at the cinema altogether?

Answer: _____ Marks: [ ] /1

4 Lily walked home from the cinema. When she had walked $\frac{3}{5}$ of the way, she stopped to tie her shoe laces. If she still had 400 m to walk, what was the total distance between the cinema and her home? Write your answer in kilometres.

Answer: _____ Marks: [ ] /1

Super Sleuth challenge

In pairs, draw a map showing the route that you think Lily might have taken between the cinema and her home. Remember to label the cinema and her home on your map, as well as the point in her journey where she stopped to tie her shoe laces. Plan your drawing with your partner and present your map to the class when you have finished.

Today's Marks: [ ] /4

Day Four Try these.

1 What fraction of the word 'FRACTION' is made up of vowels?

Top tip:
The 5 vowels are A, E, I, O and U.

Answer: | **Marks:** | /1

2 You have just 90 seconds to find as many numbers as possible that can be placed in this number sentence so that it makes sense!

$$\frac{1}{2} \text{ of } \boxed{} = \frac{1}{6} \text{ of } \boxed{}$$

Top tip:
$\frac{1}{2}$ of 10 = $\frac{1}{6}$ of 30
The number 5 is represented on each side of the equals sign.

Answer: | **Marks:** | /2

3 You have just 90 seconds to find as many numbers as possible that can be placed in this number sentence so that it makes sense!

$$\frac{1}{3} \text{ of } \boxed{} = \frac{2}{5} \text{ of } \boxed{}$$

Top tip:
$\frac{1}{3}$ of 24 = $\frac{2}{5}$ of 20
The number 8 is represented on both sides of the equals sign.

Answer: | **Marks:** | /2

Today's Marks: | /5

Duties

Reader
Calculator
Checker
Reporter

Super Sleuth investigates

Think of 3 interesting fractions questions that you could ask about the image. Swap questions with your teammates.

Do we really need fractions in life or are they just a silly part of maths class? Do you see or use fractions in your life? Discuss these questions with your team.

Total Marks: | /25 | These are examples of the maths language I used:

I used maths language during pair and group work activities. | Yes | No

10 Decimals

We are learning to: Act out investigations involving decimals. ☐ Order decimals on a number line. ☐ Solve puzzles involving decimals. ☐

Day One Study the steps used to solve the problem in the example below.

Kate, Brian and Ciara McGrath went surfing in Tramore. Kate's surfboard was 1.9 m long. Brian's was 25 cm shorter than Kate's. Ciara's was 16 cm shorter than Brian's. What was the length of Ciara's surfboard in decimal form?

CLUES

Top tip:
Round the values when estimating:
1.9 m ➜ **2 m**
2 m – 0.25 m = 1.75 m
16 cm ➜ **0.2 m**
1.75 m – **0.2 m** = 1.55 m

Circle the numbers and keywords:
1.9 m, 25 cm shorter, 16 cm shorter, decimal form

Link with operation needed (+, –, × or ÷): Subtract (–).

Use a strategy:
Visualise.

Kate 1.9 m ➜ Brian –25 cm ➜ Ciara –16 cm

Estimate and calculate:
My estimate: 1.55 m

$$\begin{array}{r} 1.90 \text{ m} \\ -0.25 \text{ m} \\ \hline 1.65 \text{ m} \end{array}$$

$$\begin{array}{r} 1.65 \text{ m} \\ -0.16 \text{ m} \\ \hline 1.49 \text{ m} \end{array}$$

Answer:
1.49 m

Summarise and check how you got your answer:
I changed the measurements to decimal form and subtracted.

Try these.

CLUES

1. The McGrath children had a sandcastle-building competition. The aim was to build the highest sandcastle they could in just 2 minutes. Below are the results. Write the decimal numbers in order from greatest to smallest.

Brian	Kate	Roisín	Clodagh	Jamie
17.7 cm	17.75 cm	17.17 cm	17.71 cm	17.07 cm

Answer: Marks: /1

2. What was the difference in height between the tallest and the shortest sandcastle? Write your answer in decimal form.

Answer: Marks: /1

Today's Marks: /2

Day Two Try these.

The following temperatures were recorded during the McGraths' holiday in Tramore:

Saturday	Sunday	Monday	Tuesday	Wednesday
21.5°C	20.7°C	21.8°C	22.9°C	21.9°C

1. What was the difference between the lowest and the highest temperature during the McGraths' holiday in Tramore?

   Answer: _____ °C Marks: ____ /1

2. The temperature in Tramore was recorded six months before the McGraths' holiday. It was $\frac{1}{3}$ of the temperature recorded on Sunday. What was the temperature?

   Answer: _____ °C Marks: ____ /1

3. On Wednesday, the temperature in Dubai was twice the temperature in Tramore. How much warmer was this than the warmest day of the McGraths' holiday?

   Answer: _____ °C Marks: ____ /1

Super Sleuth challenge

Act out one of the challenges below ten times and record your results in the tally.

- Throwing a basketball into a hoop
- Rock-paper-scissors
- Xs and Os

👍 Tally 👎	

Now, write your results in fraction and decimal form:

Fraction: ____ /10   Decimal: ____ . ____

Today's Marks: ____ /3   45

Day Three Try these.

1 Mr McGrath went shopping for a picnic. He spent €4.09 on bread, €2.50 on ham, €1.55 on cheese, €3.95 on drinks and €5 on treats. How much did he spend on cheese, bread and ham?

What surplus data can you find in question 1? Cross it out!

Estimate: [ ] Answer: [ ] Marks: [ ] /1

2 How much more did Mr McGrath spend on treats than on drinks?

Estimate: [ ] Answer: [ ] Marks: [ ] /1

3 Mr McGrath spent three times the amount that he spent on bread on a picnic basket and five times the amount that he spent on cheese on a picnic blanket. How much did he spend in total on the picnic basket and picnic blanket?

Estimate: [ ] Answer: [ ] Marks: [ ] /1

4 If Mr McGrath had the notes and coins shown below before he paid for the picnic basket and picnic blanket, how much cash did he have left?

Estimate: [ ] Answer: [ ] Marks: [ ] /1

Puzzle power

Fill in the missing values in the decimal pyramid. Use your copy to work this out.

	21.75	
		9.23
	5.59	
3.12		1.78

Today's Marks: [ ] /4

Day Four Try these.

1. In pairs, take turns being the teacher. Explain to your pupil what the difference is between 0.1 and 0.01. You can act it out or draw diagrams.

Marks: /1

2. Your pupil has handed up the homework shown. In pairs, take turns explaining why this is wrong and show your pupil how to avoid making this mistake in the future.

	4	.	3	5
+			1	.	2
	4	4	.	7

Marks: /2

3. Roisín and Jamie went to a local fairground. While there, they each spent a different amount. No digit was repeated in either amount and the two amounts combined to make €10. The amounts spent were to two decimal places, e.g. €3.48 and €6.52. What might the two amounts have been? (There is more than one answer.)

Answer: _____ Marks: /2

Today's Marks: /5

Super Sleuth investigates

Estimate and then measure the temperature in your locality at the same time on 5 consecutive days. Is there any pattern to the measurements?

	Day 1	Day 2	Day 3	Day 4	Day 5
Estimate					
Actual Temperature					

Can you invent two interesting puzzles based on the table above?

Total Marks: /14 | My favourite activity was _____

I would like to get better at _____

11 Weight

We are learning to: Rename units of weight in kg and g. ☐ Rename units of weight using decimal or fraction form. ☐ Complete a maths investigation involving weight. ☐

Day One Try these.

CLUEs

Chocolate	Strawberry	Lemon	Red velvet	Toffee
0.44 kg	408 g	0.5 kg	550 g	0.25 kg

① What is the total weight of the cakes above? Write your answer in grams.

Keywords

When we are asked to find the **total amount** of something, we must add. What other words in maths puzzles usually mean we need to add?

Estimate: **Answer:**   **Marks:** /1

② Put the weights in order, starting with the heaviest. Write your answers in grams.

Answer: **Marks:** /1

③ How much heavier is the red velvet cake than the toffee cake? Write your answer in kg using a decimal point.

Answer: **Marks:** /1

④ When Gia bought the cakes above, she had two bags to carry all five. Each bag could only hold a weight of up to 1.1 kg. How might Gia have placed the cakes into the bags, ensuring that she kept the weight in each under 1.1 kg?

Answer: **Marks:** /1

Super Sleuth challenge 💬

Choose four items from your school bag that could be easily weighed and estimate their weights. Weigh them to find out if your estimates were correct.

Strand: Measures **Strand Unit:** Weight

Today's Marks: CLUEs /4

Day Two Try these.

CLUES

- 2.5 kg
- 5.75 kg
- 10.5 kg
- 20.25 kg

Dwayne   Seth   Hunter   Seamus

- Dwayne placed 6 **yellow** weights and 4 **red** weights on his barbell.
- Seth placed 4 **green** weights on his barbell.
- Hunter placed 2 **green** weights, 2 **red** weights and 4 **yellow** weights on his barbell.
- Seamus placed 2 **blue** weights and 2 **yellow** weights on his barbell.

1 What was the total weight placed on Dwayne and Seamus's barbells?

Answer: _____ Marks: ___ /1

2 What was the difference between the weights placed on Hunter and Seth's barbells? Write your answer as a fraction of a kg.

Answer: _____ Marks: ___ /1

3 What was the total weight placed on all four barbells?

Answer: _____ Marks: ___ /1

4 In what order did the weightlifters come on competition day? Hunter lifted $1\frac{1}{2}$ kg less than Seamus, but 3.5 kg more than Seth. Seamus lifted $\frac{1}{4}$ kg more than Dwayne. Dwayne lifted 1.25 kg more than Hunter.

Answers: 1st _____ 2nd _____ 3rd _____ 4th _____ Marks: ___ /1

Today's Marks: ___ /4

49

Day Three — Try these.

CLUES

1 Molly has four younger siblings. The table below shows each child's birth weight. Write the weights in grams in the bottom row of the table.

Evie	Mia	Ben	Adam
2.9 kg	$3\frac{3}{4}$ kg	$4\frac{1}{4}$ kg	3.2 kg

Marks: /1

2 What was the total birth weight of all four babies? Write your answer in decimal form.

Answer: Marks: /1

3 What was the difference in weight between the heaviest baby and the lightest baby? Write your answer in grams.

Answer: Marks: /1

4 When Molly was born, she weighed 3,049 g. Which of her siblings was she closest to in weight?

Answer: Marks: /1

Super Sleuth challenge

As a class, each pupil must identify an item that they think weighs 1,000 g. Once you have each chosen your object, weigh it and see how close you were. The pupil who is closest to 1,000 g is the winner!

Today's Marks: /4

Day Four Try these.

Ask permission from your teacher or a parent to use the internet. You will need to use two websites to complete this activity. Use a cookery website to find a recipe for your favourite dish and use a supermarket website to research the ingredients required. Fill in the table below.

CLUES

My favourite meal is

Ingredient	① Price of ingredient in supermarket	② Weight of ingredient in supermarket	③ Weight required for recipe	④ Difference in weight
Total:				
	Marks: ___ /1	Marks: ___ /1	Marks: ___ /1	Marks: ___ /1

Today's Marks: ___ /4

Total Marks: ___ /16 | I can change weights from fractions to grams.   Yes ☐ No ☐
I can change weights from decimals to grams, e.g. 0.25 kg = 250 g.   Yes ☐ No ☐

12 Revision 2

Welcome to McGuigan's Steakhouse!

Day One

Try these.

CLUEs

1. A kid's meal at McGuigan's Steakhouse costs €6. The restaurant made €234 on kids' meals last weekend. How many kids' meals were ordered?

Answer: _____ **Marks:** ___ /1

2. The chef baked two batches of macarons. There were 256 in the first batch and 236 in the next batch. She wanted to give a free portion of 3 macarons to each of the diners at the restaurant. How many diners did she have enough portions for?

Answer: _____ **Marks:** ___ /1

3. A new waiter at the restaurant made a lot of mistakes on his first day. When serving macarons to a table of office workers, he gave 7 to Cillian, 3 to Ollie, 8 to Frances, 6 to Trevor and 11 to Leah. If they decide to share the macarons equally, how many will each person receive?

Answer: _____ **Marks:** ___ /1

4. Cillian's group were charged €14.95 for drinks, €28.75 for starters and €136.25 for main courses. The manager took €24.95 off their bill to apologise for the waiter's mistakes. How much did the meal cost per person? Break this number story down into steps to make it easier to solve.

Answer: _____ **Marks:** ___ /1

Strand: Number **Strand Units:** Operations – division; Fractions; Decimals
Strand: Measures **Strand Unit:** Weight

Today's Marks: ___ /4

Day Two Try these.

MENU

Starters

Chicken wings

Mushroom soup

Chicken Caesar salad

Main courses

Striploin steak

Rib-eye steak

Fillet steak

Fish and chips

Sirloin steak

Vegetarian stir-fry

Desserts

Cheesecake

Chocolate fudge cake

Sticky toffee pudding

---

1 What fraction of the menu above is made up of **(a)** starters and **(b)** main courses?

Answers: (a) _____ (b) _____ Marks: ___ /2

2 Which is greater: **(a)** the fraction of starters that contain chicken or **(b)** the fraction of main courses that do not contain steak? Draw diagrams below to prove that your answer is correct.

Answer: _____ Marks: ___ /1

3 If two main courses were dropped from the menu and two starters were added, what fraction of the menu would be **(a)** starters and **(b)** main courses?

Answers: (a) _____ (b) _____ Marks: ___ /2

Day Three   Try these.

1 Sophie's family visited McGuigan's Steakhouse yesterday. If Sophie ate 0.7 of her meal, how much of her meal was left uneaten? Draw a diagram to illustrate your answer.

Answer: **Marks:** /1

2 A waitress placed a jug containing 2 l of water on Sophie's table. Sophie drank 0.25 l, Richard drank 0.41 l and Jules drank 0.19 l. How many litres of water were left in the jug? Write your answer in decimal form.

Answer: **Marks:** /1

3 Mum used 0.7 l of petrol driving to the restaurant. She uses 4 times that amount of petrol driving to work. How much petrol does she use driving to and from work each day?

Answer: **Marks:** /1

4 Place the numbers below in the magic square so that all rows, columns and diagonals add up to 1.5.

| 0.1 | 0.2 | 0.3 | 0.4 | 0.5 | 0.6 | 0.7 | 0.8 | 0.9 |

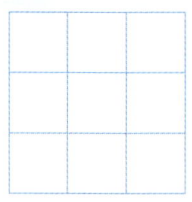

Marks: /1

Puzzle power

Use the clues to work out the missing numbers.

- The units digit is 3 times the tenths digit.
- The hundredths digit is 4 less than the units digit.
- You can make this number by taking 0.65 from 10.

U	.	$\frac{1}{10}$	$\frac{1}{100}$
	.		

Today's Marks: /4

Day Four Try these.

CLUES

1 This grid shows a steak order for a table of four at McGuigan's. What was the total weight of the steaks ordered?

Christina	Colm	Denise	Alan
227 g	0.34 kg	283 g	0.45 kg

Answer: _____ Marks: ___ /1

2 In the grid above, what was the difference in weight between the steaks ordered by the girls and the steaks ordered by the boys? Write the answer in kg with a decimal point.

Answer: _____ Marks: ___ /1

3 Which of the treats below could you combine, in any amounts, to exactly match the weight of the fruit salad?

A	B	C	Fruit salad
Millionaire square	Chocolate truffle	French fancy	
0.11 kg	48 g	27 g	0.26 kg

Answer: _____ Marks: ___ /1

Today's Marks: ___ /3

Super Sleuth challenge

The weight of the ingredients in a recipe can be changed depending on the amount of the dish that you wish to make. Using the rules below, write your own recipe for rocky road.

- You need 3 times as much **milk chocolate** as **Maltesers**.
- The **marshmallows** should weigh 75 g more than the Maltesers.
- You need the same weight of **rich tea biscuits** and **digestive biscuits**. This should be 25 g less than the weight of the milk chocolate.
- The **butter** and the marshmallows should be the same weight.

Total Marks: ___ /16

55

13 Strategy: Working Systematically

Day One

Working systematically means working in a way that helps you to organise the information in a maths story in order to solve the puzzle.

Look at the ice-cream menu below. How many different combinations of flavours are possible in a two-scoop cone?

Choose two scoops from the following flavours:		
Strawberry	Vanilla	Chocolate
Honeycomb	Raspberry	Toffee

Firstly, bear in mind that you can make 6 different cones with 2 scoops of the same flavour, so start with strawberry and pair it with each flavour, including strawberry itself. Next, pair vanilla with each flavour, including vanilla itself, but do not include strawberry, as strawberry and vanilla have already been paired. Continue pairing the flavours until all of the possible combinations are found. Making a table can help you work systematically.

Strawberry	Vanilla	Chocolate	Honeycomb	Raspberry	Toffee
Strawberry	Vanilla	Chocolate	Honeycomb	Raspberry	Toffee
Vanilla	Honeycomb	Honeycomb	Raspberry	Toffee	
Honeycomb	Chocolate	Raspberry	Toffee		
Chocolate	Raspberry	Toffee			
Raspberry	Toffee				
Toffee					

Find the number of possible combinations by counting the flavours in the bottom row of the table. There are 21 possible combinations.

Try these.

1. Senan has 4 T-shirts and 6 pairs of shorts. How many different outfits could he create by pairing each T-shirt with each pair of shorts? Act it out by drawing the T-shirts and shorts and cutting them out.

Answer: ____
Marks: ____ /1

2. Senan is sitting next to his sister Eilish and his brother Hugh. In how many different orders could they sit? Act it out.

Answer: ____
Marks: ____ /1

Today's Marks: ____ /2

Day Two Try these.

1 Eilish threw a pair of dice and added the numbers that she rolled. She got a total of 8. Find all of the totals that can be made by throwing a pair of dice. 💬

Answer: | Marks: | /1

2 Eilish had three €1 coins, three 50c coins and three 5c coins. Find all of the possible amounts of money that she could make using three of these coins.

Answer: | Marks: | /1

3 Eilish asked her dad his age. He said, "Your mum and I are in our forties. When you add our ages together, you get a total of 90. In 5 years, our ages will add up to 100! I'm 2 years older than your mum." How old is Eilish's dad?

Answer: | Marks: | /1

4 Hugh used an equal number of €20 notes, €5 notes and 50c coins to pay for a new outfit. If the cost was €178.50, how many of each note and coin did he use?

Number	€20	€5	€0.50	Total
1	€20	€5	€0.50	€25.50

Answer: | Marks: | /1

Today's Marks: | /4

Day Three Try these.

CLUEs

1 Write all of the three-digit numbers greater than 500 that can be made using the number cards below. (There are between 15 and 20 answers to this puzzle!)

| 2 | 3 | 5 | 7 | 7 |

Answer:

Marks: /1

2 Explore three different ways of adding odd numbers to make 30. Fill in the number sentences with odd numbers only.

☐ + ☐ = 30

☐ + ☐ + ☐ + ☐ = 30

☐ + ☐ + ☐ + ☐ + ☐ + ☐ = 30

Share your answers with your classmates. How many different number sentences did you find?

Marks: /3

3 Can you put the numbers 1 to 8 into the squares below so that the four calculations are correct?

☐? ÷ ☐? = ☐?

− ☐? × ☐?

☐? + ☐? = ☐?

Marks: /1

Super Sleuth challenge

The 4th Class pupils forgot to bring their football out to the yard at break time. When Nathan ran back into the classroom to get it, he knocked over Miss Desmond's notation board! 8 counters fell on the floor. Identify the numbers that might have been represented on the notation board using all 8 counters. Make sure that each section has at least one counter.

Example: The number 413 can be made using 8 counters.

H	T	U
•		
•		•
•		•
•	•	•
4	1	3

Today's Marks: /5

Day Four Try these.

Duties

Reader

Calculator

Checker

Reporter

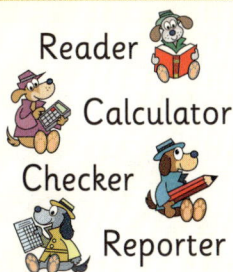

Super Sleuth's Secret Mission!

(1) The National Security Agency (NSA) is an organisation that collects information for the American Government. People who work for the NSA must be really good maths detectives, as they often have to break codes and solve puzzles. The following puzzle was inspired by a brainteaser that the NSA shared online. Can you solve it?

I have four weights. When I weigh two of them at a time, the pairs of weights add up to 6 kg, 8 kg, 10 kg, 12 kg, 14 kg and 16 kg. What might my four weights be? (There are two possible sets of answers to this puzzle.)

Top tip: This activity requires you to work systematically, while also using trial and improvement to solve the puzzle.

Answer: _____ **Marks:** ___ /1

(2) Annie threw some darts at the board shown. Every dart landed on the board and she scored exactly 100. **(a)** How many darts did she throw and **(b)** which numbers did they land on? This is an open-ended investigation with a number of possible answers.

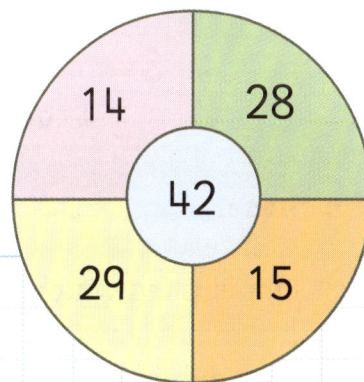

14   28

42

29   15

Answers: (a) _____ **(b)** _____ **Marks:** ___ /1

(3) Zach, Cody, Tariq, Lemar and Chang are in a boy band. They always stand in a row for publicity photographs. If Tariq always stands in the centre of photographs and Zach and Cody are always on either side of him, write all of the possible orders that the band might stand in.

Top tip: Act it out.

Marks: ___ /1

Today's Marks: ___ /3

Total Marks: ___ /14 | I can work systematically to solve maths stories.   Yes ___ No ___

One activity that I found difficult was _____

59

14 Time

We are learning to: Rename minutes as hours and hours as minutes. ☐ Read and interpret simple timetables. ☐
Solve and complete practical tasks and puzzles involving times and dates. ☐

Day One — Study the steps used to solve the problem in the example below.

Ellie finished her homework at 4:30 pm. She spent 45 minutes on her homework. At what time did she start?

CLUES

Circle the numbers and keywords:
finished at 4:30 pm, 45 minutes, start

Link with operation needed (+, −, × or ÷): None

Use a strategy: Work backwards.

Estimate and calculate:
My estimate: earlier than 4:00 pm. Count back 45 minutes.

Starts	←		←	Finishes
3:45 pm	15 mins	4:00 pm	30 mins	4:30 pm

Answer: 3:45 pm

Summarise and check how you got your answer:
I counted back 45 minutes from 4:30 pm to 3:45 pm.

Why do we break 45 minutes into 30 minutes and 15 minutes?

Try these.

CLUES

① Lily finished watching a film in the cinema at 8:15 pm. If the movie was 1 hour and 25 minutes long, at what time did it start? Show your answer on the clock face.

Film starts	←		←		←	Film ends
						8:15 pm

Marks: ☐ /2

② Harry spent 20 minutes shopping at Music World and 35 minutes shopping at The Bookworm Bookshop. If Harry left the shopping centre at 12:05 pm, at what time did he start shopping?

Starts	←		←		←	Finishes
						12:05 pm

Marks: ☐ /1

Today's Marks: ☐ /3

Day Two Try these.

1 Isla starts school at 8:50 am and finishes at 2:30 pm. How long does she spend at school? Use the timeline to count on.

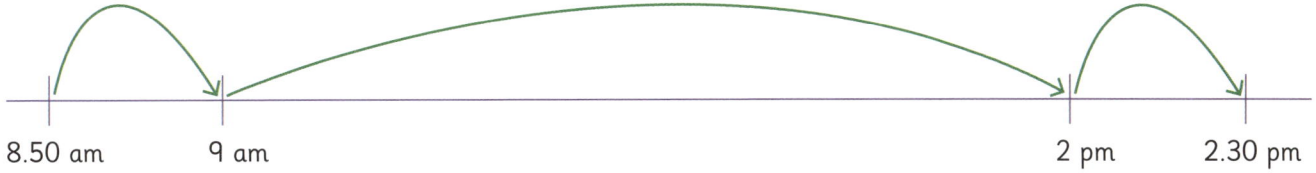

+ 10 minutes   + 5 hours   + 30 minutes

8.50 am   9 am   2 pm   2.30 pm

Answer: Marks: /1

2 Matthew's family travelled from Sligo to the Phoenix Park. If they left home at 8:35 am and the journey took two and a half hours, at what time did they arrive at the Phoenix Park?

Answer: Marks: /1

3 If Matthew's dad drove at an average speed of 80 km per hour, how far was it from their home in Sligo to the Phoenix Park?

Answer: Marks: /1

4 At 11:30 am, Matthew's family began a tour of Áras an Uachtaráin, which lasted for 1 hour and 15 minutes. Next, it took them 23 minutes to walk to Dublin Zoo, where they stopped off at a café for 45 minutes. Seven minutes later, they began a tour of the zoo. At what time did they begin their tour of the zoo?

Answer: Marks: /1

Today's Marks: /4   **61**

Day Three Try these.

APRIL						
Monday	**Tuesday**	**Wednesday**	**Thursday**	**Friday**	**Saturday**	**Sunday**
	1 April Fool's Day	2 Cake Sale	3	4 Camogie training	5 Dad's birthday	6
7 International Children's Book Day	8	9 Cumann na mBunscoil finals	10	11 Camogie training	12	13
14 Anniversary of sinking of *Titanic*	15	16	17	18 Camogie training	19	20 Easter Sunday
21	22	23	24	25 Camogie training	26 Earth Day	27
28	29	30				

1 What date is it exactly one week before International Children's Book Day?

Answer:

Marks: /1

2 If Lucy has camogie training every Friday, on what date will she have her first training session in May?

Answer:

Marks: /1

3 **(a)** What event takes place 21 days before Earth Day?

(b) How many weeks is equal to 21 days?

Answers: (a)   (b)   Marks: /2

4 **(a)** What date will it be 100 days after April 1st?

(b) How many full weeks is 100 days equal to? How many days are left over?

Answers: (a)   (b)   Marks: /2

Super Sleuth challenge

Think of one difficult challenge based on the calendar above and share it with your partner.

Today's Marks: /6

Day Four Try these.

1. Heidi won a competition to work with a zookeeper in Dublin Zoo for a day. The zookeeper sent her the following information:

The zoo opens at 9:30 am and closes at 6 pm.

You will feed the giraffes before the tigers, but after the elephants.

The tigers will eat their biggest meal 335 minutes after the zoo opens.

The meerkats will eat 75 minutes before closing time.

You will feed the elephants before midday.

Use the matrix (grid) to help you plan out Heidi's day. Tick the correct boxes.

Animal	11:20 am	1 pm	3:05 pm	4:45 pm
Meerkats				
Giraffes				
Tigers				
Elephants				

Marks: ___ /4

2. The zookeeper asked Heidi to accompany him to as many wildlife talks as possible at the various habitats. However, feeding time takes 15 minutes in each area of the zoo. Tick the talks that Heidi will be able to attend.

Habitat		Talk Begins	Duration
Red pandas		10:05 am	1 hour, 10 minutes
Reptiles		11 am	30 minutes
Penguins		Midday	45 minutes
Lemurs		1:35 pm	1 hour
Kangaroos		3:55 pm	65 minutes

Marks: ___ /5

Keywords

The **duration** of an event is how long it lasts.

Today's Marks: ___ /9

Super Sleuth challenge

In pairs, you have 30 seconds to complete each challenge! Record each other's results.

- Write your full name as many times as you can.
- Complete as many star jumps as you can.
- Say 'Tipperary' as many times as you can.
- Sing 'Happy Birthday' as many times as you can.
- Say the alphabet backwards.

Total Marks: ___ /22 | I can use a matrix to solve a problem. Yes ☐ No ☐

I can rename minutes as hours, e.g. 120 minutes = 2 hours. Yes ☐ No ☐

I can rename hours as minutes, e.g. 1 hour = 60 minutes. Yes ☐ No ☐

15 Money

We are learning to: Rename euro and cent. ☐ Use number sentences to solve puzzles. ☐

Day One — Study the steps used to solve the problem in the example below.

For Stephen's birthday, his gran gave him €45, his aunt gave him €75 and his cousin gave him €5. Stephen spent €60.95 on runners, €5.50 on a book and €1.25 on chocolate. How much did he spend altogether?

CLUES

Circle the numbers and keywords: spent, €60.95, €5.50, €1.25

Link with operation needed (+, −, × or ÷): Add (+).

Use a strategy: I used logical reasoning to eliminate the surplus data in the question.

Estimate and calculate:

My estimate:

€61 + €6 + €1 = €68

```
  €60.95
  € 5.50
+ € 1.25
  ───────
  €67.70
```

Answer: €67.70

Summarise and check how you got your answer:

I ignored the surplus data and added up the three amounts that Stephen spent.

> **Remember:** Surplus data is information that is not needed to answer the question.

Try these. **CLUES**

1. (a) Add the three values together to find the cost of the toy train. Write the answer using the € symbol and a decimal point. (b) Ben used three €2 coins to pay for this toy train. What change did he get?

304c 28c 145c

Answers: (a) _____ (b) _____ Marks: ___ /2

2. (a) Sophie has decided to save up for this bicycle. If she saves €5 a week, how many weeks will it take her to save up enough? (b) If her uncle gives her €25 for her birthday and her brother gives her €10, how many weeks will it take her to save up enough now?

€125

Answers: (a) _____ (b) _____ Marks: ___ /2

Strand: Measures **Strand Unit:** Money

Today's Marks: ___ /4

Day Two Try these.

1 Colm went to his local shop to buy some groceries. Look at his receipt. How much did he spend on bread altogether? 💬

Answer: [ ]   Marks: [ ] /1

2 How much did each apple cost? Write the answer in cent. 💬

Answer: [ ]   Marks: [ ] /1

3 How much more did he spend on chocolate than on milk? 💬

Answer: [ ]   Marks: [ ] /1

4 **(a)** Estimate and then **(b)** find the total cost of Colm's groceries. Check your work using a calculator and write the answer in cent. 💬

Answers: (a) [ ]   (b) [ ]   Marks: [ ] /1

CLUES

MOORE'S MINI MARKET

Butter	€2.96
2 cartons of milk @ €1.24 each	_____
Packet of 4 apples	€1.24
4 loaves of bread @ €1.59 each	_____
Packet of 6 buns	€1.50
3 chocolate bars @ 99c each	_____
Total:	_____

Thank you for your custom.

Super Sleuth challenge 💬

1. You have €6 to spend at Moore's Mini Market.
  ▪ What items on the receipt above would you buy?
  ▪ How much money would you have left?
  ▪ Compare your choices with your partner's.

2. Try to spend as close to €6 as possible without going over this amount.
  ▪ What items would you buy?
  ▪ How close can you come to €6?
  ▪ Share your work with your classmates.

Day Three Try these.

CLUES

What surplus data can you find in questions 1 and 3? Cross it out!

1 Mary had €32 and Anna had €48. Anna spent all of her money buying books that cost €8 each. How many books did Anna buy?

Answer: _____ Marks: ___ /1

2 Aunt Christine has two envelopes of money – one for you and one for your cousin. Envelope A contains a five-euro note and a ten-euro note. Envelope B contains nine €1 coins, eight 50c coins, seven 20c coins, six 10c coins and five 5c coins. Christine has given you the first choice. **(a)** Which envelope will you choose?
(b) What is the difference between the two amounts?

Answers: (a) _____ (b) _____ Marks: ___ /1

3 Yasmin bought three board games costing €4.50 each. Her friend Shane bought the same three games on sale at €3.75 each. Her friend Jonah bought three games and paid a total of €15. How much more in total did Yasmin pay for the games than Shane?

Answer: _____ Marks: ___ /1

4 Esmé has three times more money than Ava. Esmé has four times more money than Oisín. Oisín has €5 more than Joseph. If Ava has €8, how much do Esmé, Oisín and Joseph have altogether?

Answer: _____ Marks: ___ /1

Today's Marks: ___ /4

Day Four Try these.

Which coins or notes would you remove from the following pairs of purses to ensure that there is an equal amount of money in each? Cross out the coins or notes that you would remove.

1

A 50, 20, 50, 5

B 50, 10, 10

Marks: /1

2

A 2, 50, 2, 1, 50, 20, 5, 10

B 2, 1, 20, 1, 50, 1

Marks: /1

3

A 5 EURO, 50

B 2, 20, 5, 1, 20, 10, 2

Marks: /1

4

A 10, 1, 5 EURO, 50, 20, 2

B 2, 50, 1, 20, 10, 1, 20, 5 EURO, 5 EURO

Marks: /1

Today's Marks: /4

Total Marks: /16 | **Why is it important to learn about money?**

My favourite activity was

67

16  Capacity

We are learning to: Rename units of capacity using decimal and fraction form. ☐
Act it out to solve puzzles. ☐

Day One Study the steps used to solve the problem in the example below.

Fiona received 3 bottles of perfume for her birthday. The first contained 0.05 l, the second contained 30 ml and the third contained 0.1 l. What was the total amount of perfume? Write the answer in millilitres.

CLUES

Circle the numbers and keywords:
  3 bottles, 0.05 l, 30 ml, 0.1 l, total, millilitres

Link with operation needed (+, −, × or ÷): Add (+).

Use a strategy: Simplify by changing all to millilitres.

Estimate and calculate:

My estimate:	50 ml	Answer:
	30 ml	180 ml
less than 200 ml	+100 ml	
	180 ml	

Summarise and check how you got your answer:
  I changed the measurements to millilitres and added the three amounts together.

Keywords

Capacity
means the amount of liquid that a container can hold.

Try these.

CLUES

1. Tina drank $\frac{1}{2}$ l of milk with breakfast, 0.2 l of juice with dinner and 150 ml of hot chocolate at bedtime. What was the total amount of these three beverages? Write the answer in millilitres.

Answer: _____ Marks: ___ /1

2. Lola and her brother Bobby are having an argument. Lola thinks that **(a)** $\frac{7}{8}$ of 800 ml is greater than **(b)** $\frac{3}{4}$ of 1,000 ml, but Bobby disagrees. Which is the greater amount, **(a)** or **(b)**?

Answer: _____ Marks: ___ /1

3. An Arctic wolf drinks 31.5 l of water in 7 days. A mule deer drinks 17.1 l in 3 days. Which of these animals drinks more water per day?

Answer: _____ Marks: ___ /1

Today's Marks: ___ /3

Day Two   Try these.

CLUES

1. A power shower uses 250 l of water in 10 minutes. How much water would be used in just 1 minute?

> It is important to use water sensibly in order to protect the environment. Today's questions are based on information from Green-Schools Ireland.

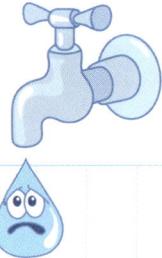

Answer: _____   Marks: ___ /1

2. A tap dripping at a rate of one drip per second wastes around 865 l of water per week. How many litres are wasted in four weeks? Use a calculator to check your work.

Answer: _____   Marks: ___ /1

3. By turning off the tap when you brush your teeth, you can save around 6 l of water. If you brush your teeth twice a day, around how many litres of water could you save in seven days?

Answer: _____   Marks: ___ /1

4. Every day, Ron and Harry both take a 5-minute power shower, while Hermione takes a 10-minute power shower. How much water do Ron and Hermione use while showering over two weeks?

> What is the surplus data in this question?

Answer: _____   Marks: ___ /1

Super Sleuth investigates

How much water could be saved each day if:

1. every child in your class reduced their water usage by 500 ml per day?
2. every child in your school reduced their water usage by 1 l per day?

Day Three Try these.

Use the containers in the table below to complete the questions that follow. You can use the same container more than once. Change all of the capacities to decimal form to make your work easier.

Top tip: Act it out.

A	B	C	D	E
0.5 l	1.25 l	$\frac{3}{4}$ l	1,000 ml	$\frac{1}{10}$ l

1 Which of the containers above would you use to measure out 1.85 l of water into a basin?

Answer: ___ Marks: ___ /1

2 Which of the containers above would you use to measure out 2.7 l of water into a basin?

Answer: ___ Marks: ___ /1

3 Which of the containers above would you use to measure out 5.35 l of water into a basin?

Answer: ___ Marks: ___ /1

4 Think of at least five ways in which you could measure out 2,000 ml of water into a basin using these containers.

Answer: ___ Marks: ___ /1

Puzzle power

Pavel needs exactly 500 ml of water to make porridge, but he doesn't have a measuring jug. He has two empty bottles that hold 1 l and 750 ml. How can he use these to measure out exactly 500 ml of water?

Today's Marks: ___ /4

Day Four | Try these.

1 Jasmine has invited three friends to go hiking with her. She decides that they should each drink 650 ml of water. If she brings a 2 l bottle and a 500 ml bottle of water, will this be enough for each child to drink 650 ml?

Answer: _____ **Marks:** ___ /1

2 If Peter uses 25 ml of washing-up liquid each day, for how long will a 350 ml bottle last?

350ml

Answer: _____ **Marks:** ___ /1

3 Kim uses 15 ml of shampoo and 20 ml of conditioner every time she washes her hair. If the shampoo bottle contains 180 ml and the conditioner bottle contains 260 ml, which will run out first?

Answer: _____ **Marks:** ___ /1

Today's Marks: ___ /3

Super Sleuth investigates

Explain what has gone wrong for Leo and Taylor.

Leo, can you get me 100 ml of milk, please?

Chef asked you for 100 ml of milk, not 120 ml!

500
400
300
200
100

Total Marks: ___ /14 | I can rename units of capacity as litres or millilitres. **Yes** ☐ **No** ☐

I can act it out to solve puzzles. **Yes** ☐ **No** ☐

17 Lines and Angles

We are learning to: Identify, describe and classify lines and angles. ☐
Draw, discuss and describe intersecting lines and their angles. ☐

Day One Look at the types of line below.

Horizontal	Vertical	Diagonal or Oblique	Parallel Lines	Perpendicular Lines

Try these.

You will need a set square for the drawing activities in this unit.

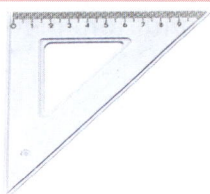

CLUES

1. How would you explain to a younger child how they should draw two lines, perpendicular to one another, as accurately as possible? Write your step-by-step approach and use it to draw your own perpendicular lines.

My perpendicular lines

Marks: ☐ /1

2. Draw examples of each of the following lines found in your school:

Horizontal	Vertical	Diagonal or Oblique	Parallel Lines	Perpendicular Lines

Marks: ☐ /5

Strand: Shape and Space **Strand Unit:** Lines and Angles

Today's Marks: ☐ /6

Day Two Try these.

CLUES

1. Write one example of the following types of line found in the image above:

Horizontal	Vertical	Diagonal or Oblique	Parallel Lines	Perpendicular Lines

Marks: /5

2. Write three examples of the following types of angle found in the image above:

Less than a Right Angle	Right Angle	Greater than a Right Angle

Marks: /9

3. In your copy, draw a bird's-eye view of your classroom. Use the words 'parallel', 'perpendicular' and 'diagonal' to describe the position of a few items in relation to others, e.g. My desk is parallel to the nature table.

Marks: /3

Super Sleuth investigates

Use an encyclopaedia or the internet (ask permission first) to find national flags that include the details listed below. (There are many possible answers.)

1. Three horizontal bars of different colours
2. One blue horizontal line and one blue vertical line on a background of a different colour
3. A red diagonal line
4. More than 16 acute angles
5. Two angles less than a right angle and two angles greater than a right angle

Today's Marks: /17   73

Day Three Try these.

Clues

Make a homemade protractor using geostrips, pipe cleaners or two strips of cardboard connected by a paper fastener. You can use this to measure an angle to see if it is an acute angle, a right angle or an obtuse angle.

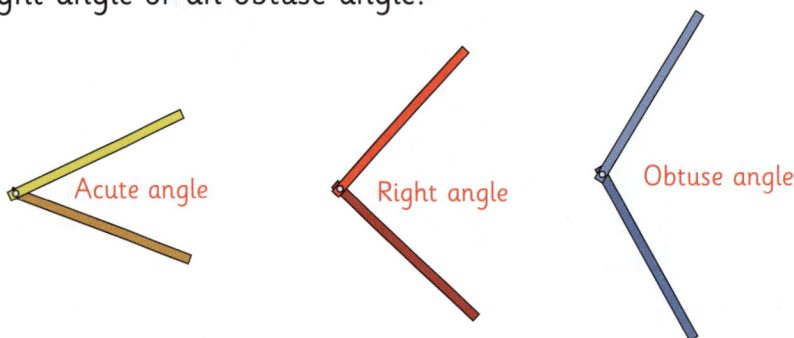

Acute angle   Right angle   Obtuse angle

1 Choose three items in your classroom. You will investigate the type of angle in each of these. List your three items in the table below and estimate whether they contain an acute angle, a right angle or an obtuse angle. Use your homemade protractor and a set square to measure the angle in each of your chosen items.

Item	Estimated Angle	Real Angle
Laptop	The screen appears to be at a right angle to the keyboard.	I discovered that it was an acute angle.

Marks: /6

2 The letters in the table below were placed in categories based on something they have in common in terms of lines or angles. Can you work out what the name of each category might be?

Category	Letters
	E F H N
	V A Z
	T L
	X K M W

Marks: /4

74

Today's Marks: /10

Day Four Try these.

Looking at the paintings below, you can see that the Dutch artist, Piet Mondrian, was very much inspired by lines and angles.

Lozenge Composition with Yellow, Black, Blue, Red and Grey by Piet Mondrian (1921)

Composition with Yellow, Blue and Red by Piet Mondrian (1937–1942)

1 How many right angles can you count in the first painting above? Justify your answer with an explanation.

Answer: **Marks:** ☐ /1

2 Use a pencil, a ruler and a set square to draw a shape with 12 lines and at least 8 right angles. Discuss the strategy that you used to create your shape. 🗨

Marks: ☐ /2

Today's Marks: ☐ /3

Super Sleuth challenge

Create your own lines-and-angles artwork, taking Piet Mondrian's paintings as your inspiration. In groups, display your completed artwork and use maths language to describe the lines and angles that you have used.

Total Marks: ☐ /36 | In this unit, I did very well at _____

I would like to improve at _____

18 Revision 3

Forest Park Summer Camp

Day One Try these.

Activity	Time
Roll call	9:30 am
Arts and crafts	9:45 am
Break	10:15 am
Horse riding	10:30 am
Orienteering	11:15 am
Lunch	12:30 pm
Canoeing	1:30 pm
Home time	3:00 pm

CLUEs

1 Look at the timetable for Monday at the Forest Park Summer Camp. How long is it from the start of arts and crafts until home time? Write the answer as hours and minutes.

Answer: _____ Marks: ___ /1

2 Four children participated in the orienteering activity. The winner was the participant who completed the course in the fastest time. Fill in the missing times and durations below and find out who the winner was. Tick the winner's name.

Participant		Starting Time	Finishing Time	Duration
Hope		11:16 am	12:02 pm	
Bob		11:19 am		42 minutes
Faith			12:10 pm	41 minutes
Sven		11:31 am	12:09 pm	

Marks: ___ /1

3 Bob left the camp at 10:30 am to go to the dentist and returned at 11:05 am. Not including roll call, break, lunch or his visit to the dentist, how long did he spend at the activities throughout the day? Write the answer as hours and minutes.

Answer: _____ Marks: ___ /1

Strand: Measures **Strand Units:** Time; Money; Capacity
Strand: Shape and Space **Strand Unit:** Lines and Angles

Today's Marks: ___ /3

Day Two Try these.

CLUEs

An ice-cream van came to the camp on Friday. Below is the price list.

Ice-cream Cone	Popcorn	Candy Floss	Slushie	Soft Drink
€1.50	95c	€1.15	€1.25	€1.05

1 Nisa paid for an item above using €2 and received 85c in change. What item did she buy?

Answer: ____ Marks: __ /1

2 Nisa then decided to buy an ice-cream cone and a soft drink. What was the total amount that she spent at the ice-cream van that day?

Answer: ____ Marks: __ /1

3 What three items could you buy for exactly €3.45?

Answer: ____ Marks: __ /1

4 Jamie spent a total of €10.35 on ice-cream cones and popcorn. Can you work out how many of each he bought? You could make a table and use trial and improvement to help you solve this.

Answer: ____ Marks: __ /1

Super Sleuth investigates

If you had €2 to spend at the ice-cream van, what would you choose to buy? How much change would you receive?

Day Three Try these.

1 Edel the cookery teacher showed the children how to make fruit punch. She used 0.85 l of orange juice, 10 ml of lemon juice and $\frac{1}{4}$ l of cranberry juice. What was the total amount of liquid? Write the answer in ml.

Answer: _____ Marks: ___ /1

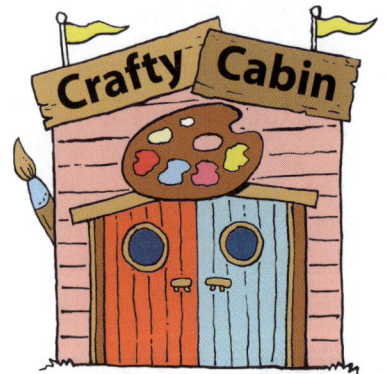

2 Finn's uncle Harry used 2.5 l of petrol driving Finn to the camp on Friday. Harry had to drive the same distance four times (two return journeys). If petrol costs €1.20 per litre, how much did the petrol for the journeys cost?

Answer: _____ Marks: ___ /1

3 Nina needs to buy paint for the arts and crafts classes. If 100 ml of paint costs 50c, how much would 1.5 l of paint cost?

Crafty Cabin

Answer: _____ Marks: ___ /1

4 The camp has three swimming pools named after famous pirate ships. The *Fortune* holds half the amount of water that the *Tiger* holds. The *Tiger* holds 2,754 l more water than the *Revenge*. If the *Revenge* holds 6,370 l, how much water do **(a)** the *Fortune* and **(b)** the *Tiger* hold?

Answers: (a) _____ (b) _____ Marks: ___ /2

Super Sleuth challenge

Nina has 3 bottles of **green** paint and 2 bottles of **yellow** paint in the Crafty Cabin. In your copy, draw as many different ways of placing the bottles in a line as possible. Use logical reasoning to help you.

Today's Marks: ___ /5

Day Four Try these.

Map of Forest Park Summer Camp

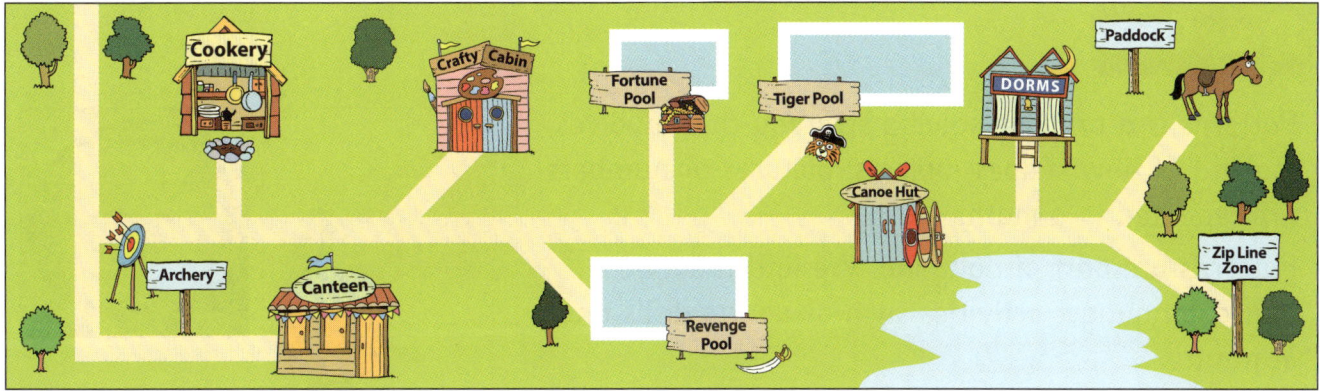

For each of the following, write a sentence about the map that includes the keyword.

1 Horizontal: _____

_____ Marks: ___ /1

2 Vertical: _____

_____ Marks: ___ /1

3 Diagonal: _____

_____ Marks: ___ /1

4 Right angle: _____

_____ Marks: ___ /1

5 Parallel: _____

_____ Marks: ___ /1

6 Perpendicular: _____

_____ Marks: ___ /1

Today's Marks: ___ /6

Super Sleuth investigates

Adil has lost his map of the camp. In pairs, explain how you would give him directions using maths language.

1. He needs to go from the Canteen to the Crafty Cabin.

2. He needs to go from the Crafty Cabin to the Canoe Hut.

3. He needs to go from the Canoe Hut to the Zip Line Zone.

Total Marks: ___ /18

19 Strategy: Patterns

Day One

Patterns is a problem-solving strategy that involves looking at how shapes, objects, pictures or numbers are repeated in a maths story.

Patterns are part of daily life. We find them in music, language, activities such as sports drills and in nature.

This limerick has a rhyming pattern of AABBA:

There was an old teacher in school,	A
And he thought he was really cool,	A
All day he would sing,	B
He got a nose ring,	B
The children they did ridicule!	A

When we look at a pattern, we can figure out the rule that created it and predict what will happen next. Look at the following number sequence:

$$3, 9, 27, \underline{\quad}, \underline{\quad}, \underline{\quad}.$$

Each term is multiplied by 3 ($3 \times 3 = 9$, $9 \times 3 = 27$ and so on), meaning that the rule is the number × 3.

Try these.

Top tip: When describing a pattern, remember to be as specific as possible with your maths language.

1. Complete the number sequence below. The rule is the decimal + 0.75.

   0.03, ____, ____, ____.

   Answer: _____ Marks: __ /1

2. Complete the number sequence below. The rule is the decimal − 0.04.

   5.1, ____, ____, ____.

   Answer: _____ Marks: __ /1

3. Move the long hand of the clock 15 minutes in an anticlockwise direction each time.

   Marks: __ /1

Today's Marks: __ /3

Day Two   Try these.

1 Analyse the pattern below. Find the rule and continue the pattern.

Z1, Y2, X3, _____, _____, _____.

Rule: _____   Marks: ___ /2

2 Analyse the number sequence below. Find the rule and continue the number sequence.

18, 19, 15, 16, 12, 13, _____, _____, _____.

Rule: _____   Marks: ___ /2

3 Analyse the pattern below. Find the rule and continue the pattern.

Rule: _____   Marks: ___ /2

4 Analyse the pattern below. Find the rule and complete the pattern.

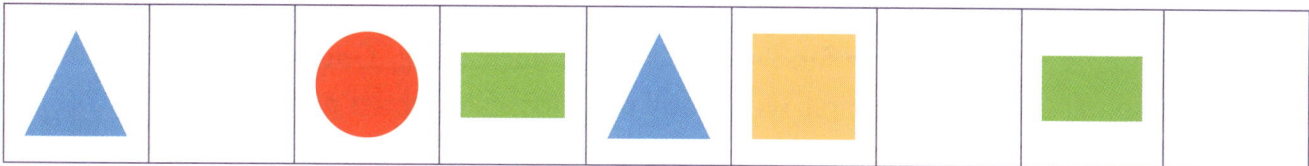

Rule: _____   Marks: ___ /2

Puzzle power

For every 3 computer games that Beth played, Ann played 5. If they played 112 games between them, how many did each child play? Use the table to find the answer. Remember: You don't need to fill in every box to get the final answer.

Beth	3	6												
Ann	5	10												
Total														

Day Three Try these.

CLUES

1 Gavin and Sadie set up a business producing flip-flops. Their flip-flops became so popular that they sold double the amount plus 5 extra pairs each week. Can you fill in the rest of their sales?

July 8th	July 15th	July 22nd	July 29th	August 5th	August 12th
2	9				

Marks: /1

2 Gavin and Sadie earned a lot of money from their business. As each week went by, the money trebled (times 3) minus €1.50. Can you work out how much money they earned each week? Use a calculator to solve this puzzle.

July 8th	July 15th	July 22nd	July 29th	August 5th	August 12th
€5	€13.50				

Marks: /1

3 From August 12th, sales of flip-flops decreased each week. Gavin and Sadie lost €55 in the first week, but their losses doubled each week. On what date did Gavin and Sadie make just €208.50?

Top tip: Make a table.

Answer: _____ Marks: /1

Puzzle power

The flip-flop business grew rapidly during July. Can you think of a reason why the sales increased as they did?

Turn the shape in a clockwise direction three more times.

Today's Marks: /3

Day Four Try these.

1 Continue the next three shapes in this pattern and write the number of circles in each shape.

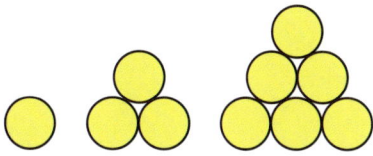

Marks: /1

2 Identify the rule and continue the pattern.

Marks: /1

3 Draw your own pattern using the three boxes. The rule is add one smiley face and take away one triangle each time.

Marks: /1

4 Draw or write your own pattern using the three boxes. The rule is subtract 80 minutes each time.

Marks: /1

Super Sleuth challenge

Today's Marks: /4

Create two pattern puzzles to share with your partner, using your work in this unit as your inspiration.

Total Marks: /18 | Identify three patterns in your home or garden that you observed this week.

The most important thing that I learned in this unit was

We are learning to: Identify, describe and classify 2-D shapes. ☐ Construct and draw 2-D shapes using a ruler and a set square. ☐ Combine, tessellate and make patterns using 2-D shapes. ☐

Day One   **Try these.**   Remember to use a pencil, a ruler and a set square throughout this unit.

CLUE**s**

1. Draw three different types of triangle. Write two short facts about each. Label the measurements on each side of the triangles.

Name			
Diagram			
Fact 1			
Fact 2			

Marks: ___ /3

2. Describe the differences between a regular pentagon and an irregular pentagon. Draw both shapes to help with your explanation.

_____

_____

Regular Pentagon	Irregular Pentagon

Marks: ___ /2

Today's Marks: C**LUE**s /5

Day Two Try these.

Use the clues below to figure out what 2-D shape is being described. Write the name of the shape and draw a picture of it.

1 I am a 2-D shape with 5 sides and 5 angles. My sides are different lengths. My angles are different sizes.

I am an

_____ .

Draw me.

Marks: ☐ /2

2 I have three pairs of parallel lines. All of my sides are the same length. I have more sides than a pentagon, but fewer sides than an octagon.

I am a

_____ .

Draw me.

Marks: ☐ /2

3 I am a quadrilateral. All of my sides are equal in length. I have two pairs of parallel lines. I do not have any right angles.

I am a

_____ .

Draw me.

Marks: ☐ /2

4 Two of my sides are the same length. Two of my angles are the same size. I have no parallel lines. My angles add up to 180°.

I am an

_____ .

Draw me.

Marks: ☐ /2

Today's Marks: ☐ /8

85

Day Three Try these.

1 Describe in your own words what the word 'tessellation' means. Draw a diagram to help with your explanation.

Diagram

Marks: ☐ /2

2 Create your own tessellating pattern.

Marks: ☐ /1

3 Continue the tessellating pattern below.

Marks: ☐ /1

I think that circles are perfect for tessellation!

Jim

4 Explain whether you agree or disagree with Jim's statement above. Draw a diagram to help with your explanation.

Diagram

Marks: ☐ /2

Today's Marks: ☐ /6

Day Four Try these. CLUEs

1. What would the 16th shape in this pattern be?
Use logical reasoning to help you. Explain your answer.

Answer: _____ **Marks:** ☐ /1

2. Mrs Clarke's class chose their favourite 2-D shapes. Figure out which child chose each shape using the matrix (grid) below. Tick the answers.

- Serena's favourite shape has more than 4 sides.
- Dimitri's favourite shape has four pairs of parallel lines.
- Ryan's favourite shape has two pairs of parallel lines and all of its sides are the same length.
- Simone does not like shapes that have sides of equal length.

	Scalene Triangle	Regular Pentagon	Rhombus	Regular Octagon
Dimitri				
Ryan				
Serena				
Simone				

Marks: ☐ /4

3. Using the clues below, figure out the shapes and the order in which they should be placed in the table. 🗨

- The 1st and 2nd shapes have a total of 11 sides.
- The 2nd and 3rd shapes have a total of 12 sides.
- The 3rd and 4th shapes have a total of 9 sides.
- The 1st and 4th shapes have a total of 8 sides.
- The 3rd shape has half as many sides as the 2nd shape.

Top tip:
You are using logical reasoning to solve today's puzzles!

Draw the four shapes in the correct order and label them.

1st Shape	2nd Shape	3rd Shape	4th Shape

Marks: ☐ /1

Today's Marks: ☐ /6

Total Marks: ☐ /25 | I can explain what the word 'tessellation' means. Yes ☐ No ☐

I can use my pencil, ruler and set square to draw 2-D shapes. Yes ☐ No ☐

21 Area

Day One

Area measures the size of a surface. This is a square centimetre (1 cm²):
The square measures 1 centimetre on each side.

Try these.

Important note:
In the diagrams in this entire unit, each square represents 1 cm².

CLUES

1 What is the area of this shape?

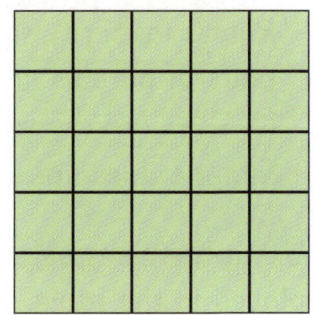

Answer: _____ cm² Marks: ___ /1

2 What is the area of the shaded part of this shape?

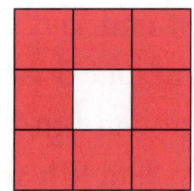

Answer: _____ cm² Marks: ___ /1

3 What is the area of this shape?

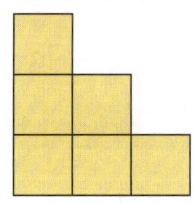

Answer: _____ cm² Marks: ___ /1

4 If you added two rows to this shape and removed three columns, what would the area of the new shape be?

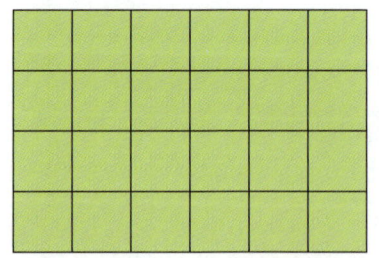

Answer: _____ cm² Marks: ___ /1

Top tip:
Rows travel horizontally while columns travel vertically.

		c	
r	o	w	
		l	
		u	
		m	
		n	

Strand: Measures **Strand Unit:** Area

Today's Marks: ___ /4

Day Two Try these.

Top tip: Some shapes contain squares that are half shaded. Remember that $2 \times \frac{1}{2}$ cm^2 = 1 cm^2.

CLUES

1 Find the area of each of the shapes below. Estimate first.

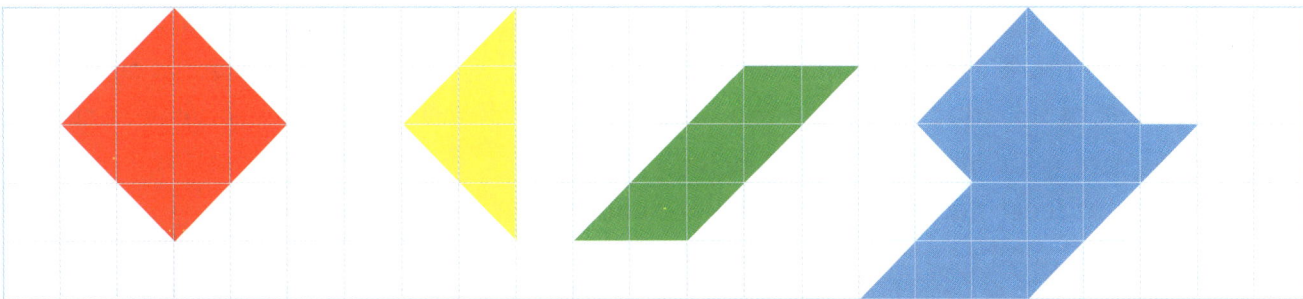

Shape	Red	Yellow	Green	Blue
Estimate	cm²	cm²	cm²	cm²
Area	cm²	cm²	cm²	cm²

Marks: /4

2 Put the shapes above in order starting with the one with the smallest area.

	1	2	3	4
Shape				

Marks: /1

3 What is the total area of the shapes above?

Answer: _____ cm² Marks: /1

4 By drawing just one straight line, can you divide shape B below in order to create a section that has the same area as shape A? (There is more than one answer.)

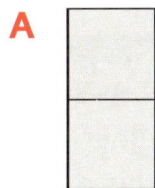

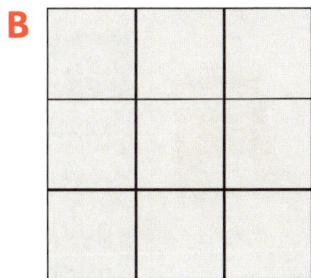

A

B

Marks: /1

Today's Marks: /7   89

Day Three Try these.

1 Find the area of the parallelogram below.

Here are some tips to help you:

Top tip: Some shapes contain squares that are partially shaded. If more than half of a square is shaded, it is counted as 1 cm². If less than half is shaded, do not count the square at all.
Remember that $2 \times \frac{1}{2}$ cm² = 1 cm².

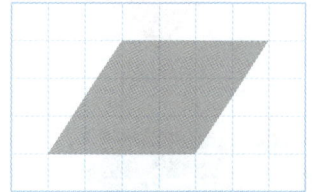

- Firstly, count the full squares. Use your pencil to mark each full square. Write the number of full squares beside the diagram.
- Next, use your pencil to mark each square that is at least half shaded. These are counted as 1 cm². Write the number beside the diagram.
- Are there any half squares that can be combined to make full squares? If so, write the number beside the diagram.
- Add the numbers that you have written beside the diagram to find the area of the parallelogram.

Answer: _____ cm² Marks: ___ /1

2 What is the approximate area of this shape?

Answer: _____ cm² Marks: ___ /1

3 What is the approximate area of this shape?

Answer: _____ cm² Marks: ___ /1

Super Sleuth challenge

Bonnie is feeling very confident in what she has learned about area. Discuss with your partner if you think Bonnie's calculation is correct or incorrect. Give reasons for your answer.

The area of my notebook is 50 m².

Super Sleuth investigates

Mark out 1 m² in your classroom. Using this as a guide, can you estimate what might measure 50 m²?

Today's Marks: ___ /3

Day Four Try these.

You will need a sheet of paper (coloured is best), a pencil, a ruler and a pair of scissors to do some detective work in this activity.

CLUES

1 Using a pencil and a ruler, draw a grid of 18 squares that each measure 1 cm^2 on the sheet of paper. Carefully cut out the squares. How many different rectangles with an area of 18 cm^2 can you make using the 18 pieces of paper? Record your findings in the table below.

	Length	Width	Area
Rectangle 1	cm	cm	cm^2
Rectangle 2	cm	cm	cm^2
Rectangle 3	cm	cm	cm^2

Marks: /3

2 Using a bird's-eye view, design a plan of a classroom on 1 cm^2 paper. Use a scale of 1 cm^2 = 1 m^2. Measure the area of the items listed in the table by counting the squares.

Item	Area
Pupil's desk	
Teacher's desk	
Library	
Total floor area	

Duties

Reader
Calculator
Checker
Reporter

Marks: /4

3 Use 1 cm^2 paper to measure the area of three items in your classroom or home. Record your findings in the table.

Item	Estimate	Area

Marks: /3

Today's Marks: /10

Total Marks: /24 | **Area means**

During this unit, I discovered

91

22 Symmetry

We are learning to: Identify line symmetry in the environment. ☐ Identify lines of symmetry as horizontal, vertical or diagonal. ☐ Complete the missing half of a shape, picture or pattern in drawings. ☐

Day One

A 2-D shape is symmetrical if a line can be drawn through it, making one side a mirror image of the other. The line is called a line of symmetry. A line of symmetry can be vertical, horizontal or diagonal.

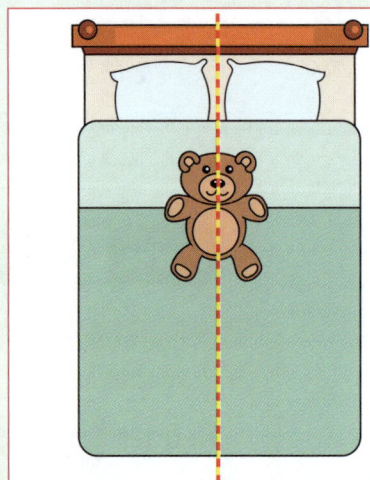

| Vertical line of symmetry | Horizontal line of symmetry | Diagonal line of symmetry |

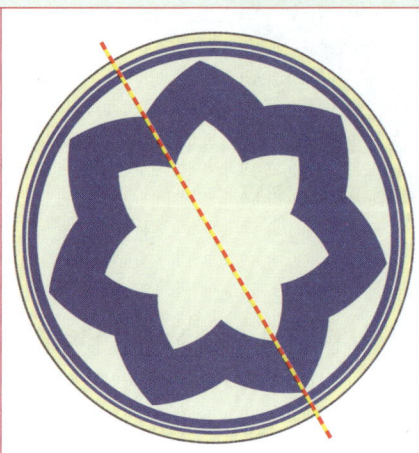

Try these.

CLUES

1. Identify three items in your classroom with no line of symmetry.

   (a)　　　　　　　　(b)　　　　　　　　(c)

   Marks: ☐ /3

2. Identify three items in your classroom that have both a horizontal and a vertical line of symmetry. Draw and label the items in the boxes below. Remember to draw the lines of symmetry.

   Marks: ☐ /3

3. This is one-quarter of Izzy's drawing. Is there more than one way to complete this picture? Choose a method, complete the picture and colour it in. 💬

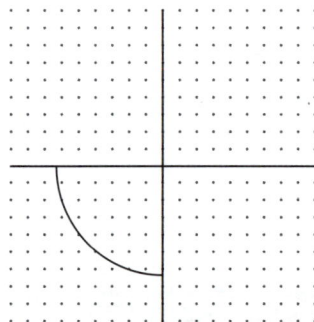

   Marks: ☐ /2

Strand: Shape and Space **Strand Unit:** Symmetry

Today's Marks: ☐ /8

Day Two Try these.

Complete the following pictures, ensuring that they are symmetrical in both shape and colour.

1

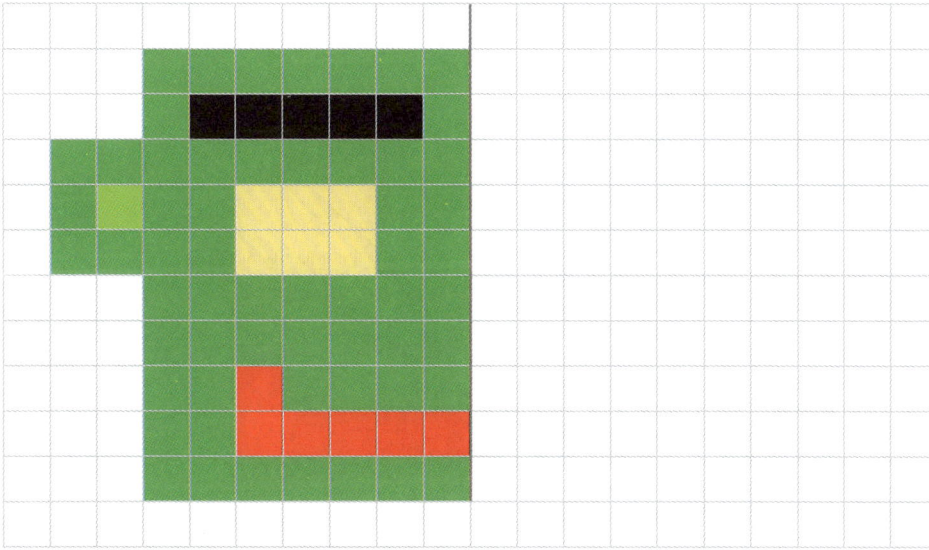

Marks: /1

2

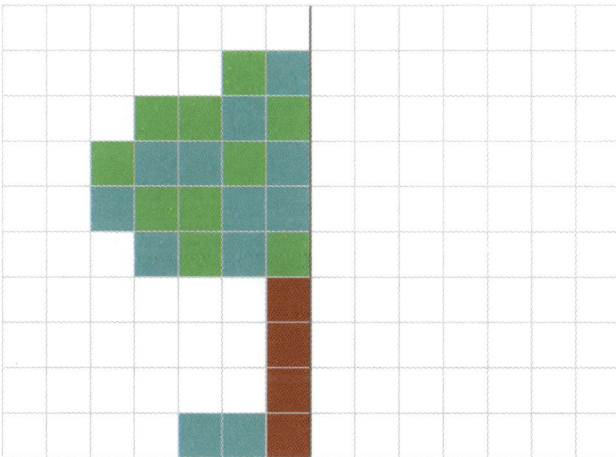

Marks: /1

3

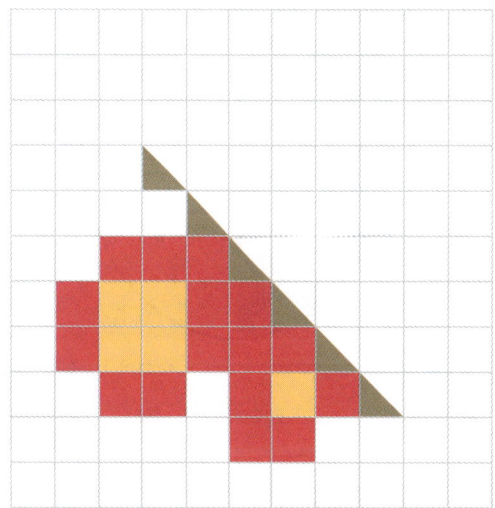

Marks: /1

4

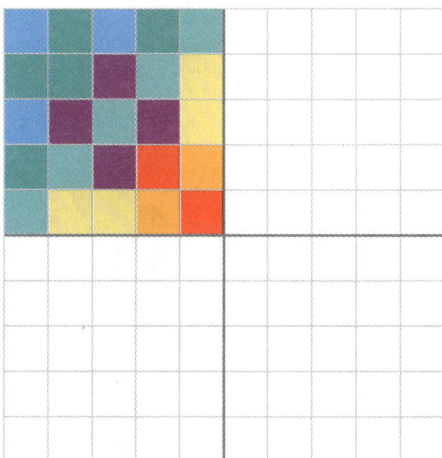

Marks: /1

Today's Marks: /4

Day Three Try these.

Name the line of symmetry used in each of the following shapes and complete the images.

1

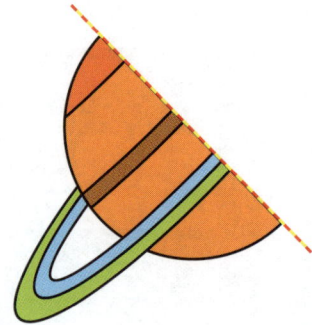

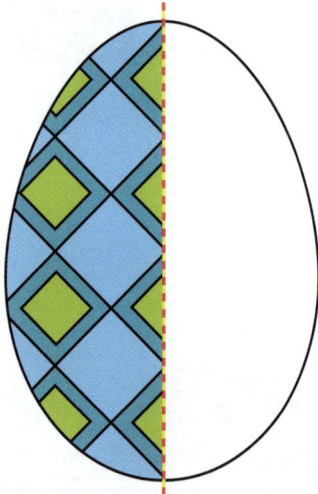

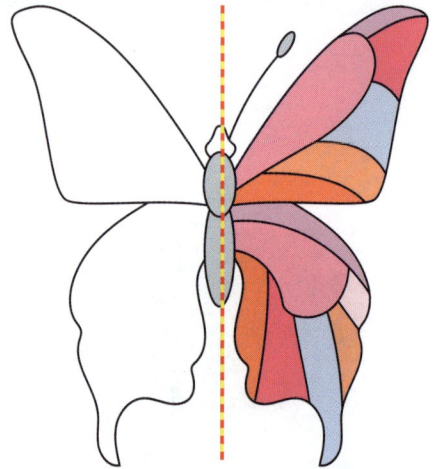

Answer: ___ Marks: ___ /1

2

Answer: ___ Marks: ___ /1

3

Answer: ___ Marks: ___ /1

4

Answer: ___ Marks: ___ /1

Puzzle power

Which one of the options below is the mirror image of this shape?

Discuss your answer with your partner and justify your choice.

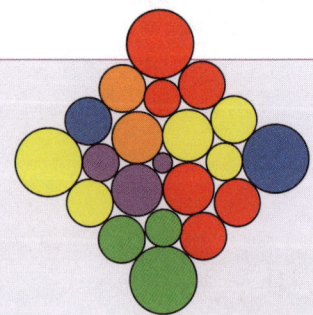

A	B	C	D

Today's Marks: ___ /4

Day Four Try these.

1. Look at the shapes. Three of the people below are telling a lie. Who is telling the truth? Tick the answer.

"All of these shapes have 3 lines of symmetry each."	"The second shape does not have any lines of symmetry."	"Two of these shapes have 4 lines of symmetry each."	"These shapes have no lines of symmetry."
Frankie	**Claire**	**Sadiq**	**Summer**

Marks: ☐ /1

2. Find an example of each of the following in your classroom:

(a) A vertical line of symmetry	**(b)** A horizontal line of symmetry	**(c)** A diagonal line of symmetry	**(d)** More than one line of symmetry

Marks: ☐ /4

3. Be the teacher! For homework, Joe was asked to complete a shape symmetrically and was given the white shape shown below to help get him started. Correct Joe's homework. If you think he made an error, draw what you think is the correct answer.

Joe's Answer

My Answer

Marks: ☐ /1

Today's Marks: ☐ /6

Total Marks: ☐ /22

I can identify horizontal, vertical and diagonal lines of symmetry.   Yes ☐ No ☐

I can complete the missing half of a picture or pattern where the line of symmetry is vertical, horizontal or diagonal.   Yes ☐ No ☐

23 🐺 3-D Shapes

We are learning to: Use a Venn diagram to classify 3-D shapes. ☐ Investigate the properties of prisms. ☐
Construct 3-D shapes. ☐

Day One

Examples of 3-D shapes:

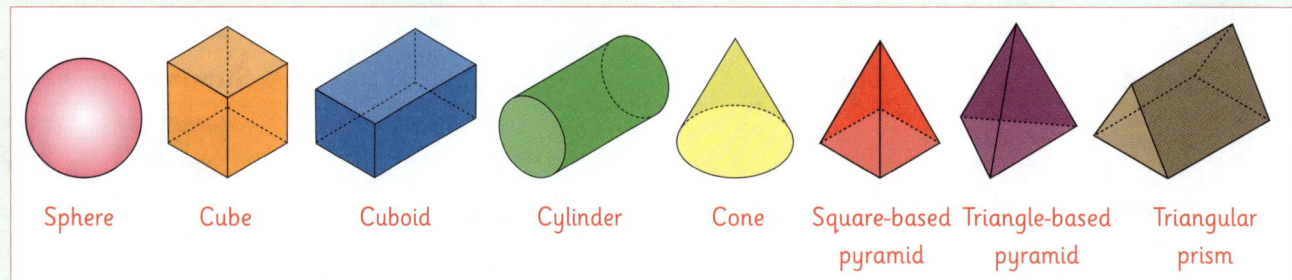

| Sphere | Cube | Cuboid | Cylinder | Cone | Square-based pyramid | Triangle-based pyramid | Triangular prism |

A prism is a 3-D shape with two identical ends. Its other faces are flat shapes. If you slice evenly through a prism to make a cross section as shown, each face is equal in shape and size. Can you identify the prisms above?

Try these.

CLUES

1 **(a)** This shape has 2 faces: one curved and one flat. Its flat face is a circle. What is it? **(b)** Where might you see this shape in real life?

Answers: (a) _____ (b) _____ Marks: __ /2

2 **(a)** This shape has 6 flat faces, 12 edges and 8 vertices. All of its faces are square. What is it? **(b)** Where might you find this shape in real life?

Keywords

A **vertex** (plural **vertices**) is a corner on a 3-D shape. This is where its edges meet.

Answers: (a) _____ (b) _____ Marks: __ /2

3 **(a)** This shape has 6 vertices, 9 edges and 5 flat faces. A cross section of this shape is equal in shape and size throughout the length of the shape. What is it? **(b)** Where might you find this shape in real life?

Answers: (a) _____ (b) _____ Marks: __ /2

4 **(a)** This shape has 5 flat faces. Four of them are triangles. It has 5 vertices and 8 edges. It is not a prism. It cannot be stacked. What is it? **(b)** Where might you find this shape in real life?

Answers: (a) _____ (b) _____ Marks: __ /2

Today's Marks: ___ /8

Day Two Try these.

1 If you were to dip a triangular prism into paint and make a print of all of its faces, you would end up with prints of two different 2-D shapes. How many prints of each 2-D shape would you have?

Answer: _____ Marks: ____ /2

2 Copy the shape using a pencil and a ruler. Fill in the blanks.

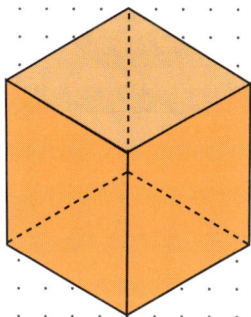

This shape is called a _____ . It

has _____ faces, which are all

_____ . It has ____ edges and

____ vertices.

Marks: ____ /6

3 Copy the shape using a pencil and a ruler. Fill in the blanks.

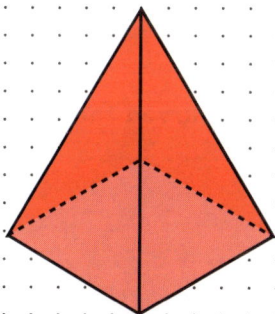

This shape is called a _____

_____ . It has

____ faces, which are _____

and _____ .

It has ____ edges and ____ vertices.

Marks: ____ /7

4 Four 3-D shapes are arranged in a row. Using the clues below, can you work out the order in which the shapes are arranged? Use logical reasoning to solve this puzzle.

- Shapes A and B have a total of 7 faces.
- Shapes B and C have a total of 8 faces.
- Shapes C and D have a total of 9 faces.
- Shapes A and D have a total of 8 faces.

A	B	C	D

Answer: _____ Marks: ____ /1

Today's Marks: ____ /16

Day Three   Try these.

CLUES

1 A Venn diagram is used for sorting information into different categories. Use this Venn diagram to fill in the table below.

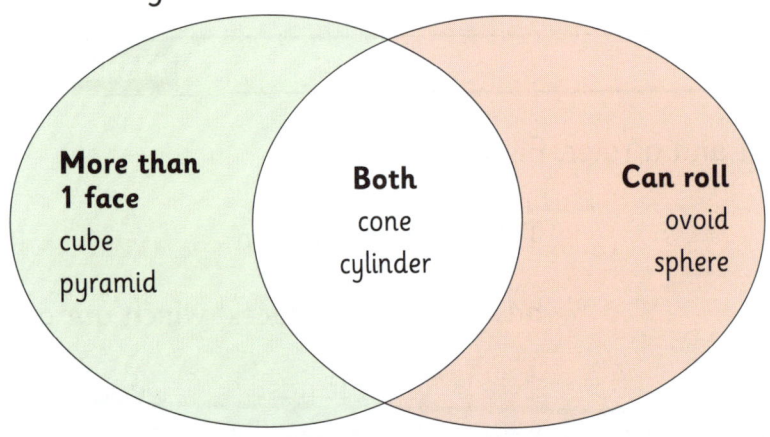

More than 1 face
cube
pyramid

Both
cone
cylinder

Can roll
ovoid
sphere

Keywords

An **ovoid** is a 3-D shape that looks like an egg.

More than 1 face only	More than 1 face and can roll	Can roll only

Marks: ____ /6

2 Place each 3-D shape in the most suitable category.

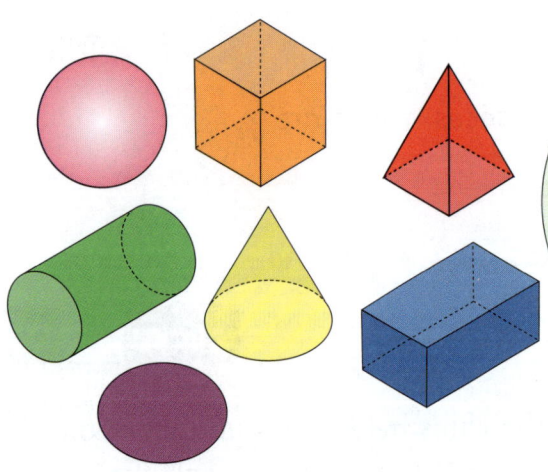

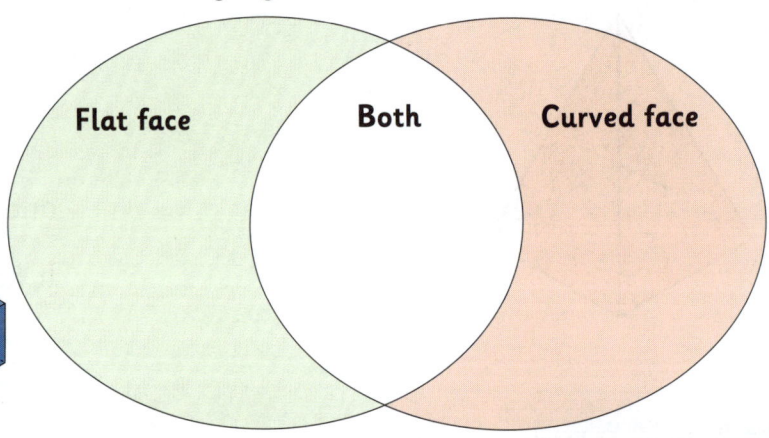

Flat face   **Both**   **Curved face**

Marks: ____ /7

3 Place each 3-D shape in the most suitable category.

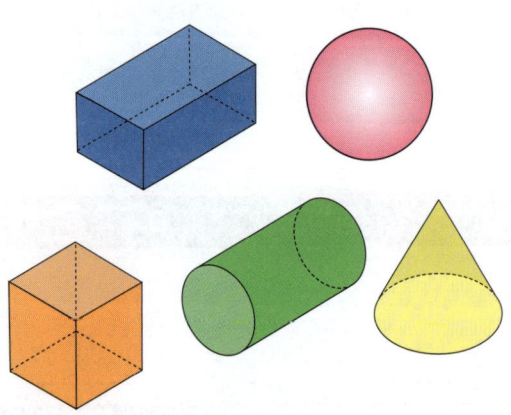

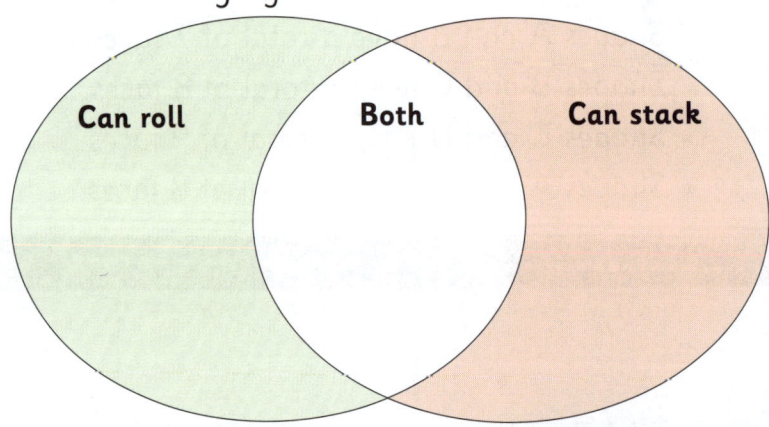

Can roll   **Both**   **Can stack**

Marks: ____ /5

Today's Marks: ____ /18

Day Four Try these.

① Other than an egg, can you think of two examples of ovoid objects in real life?

Answer: _____ Marks: ___ /1

② Alannah's treehouse is made up of two different 3-D shapes, but none of her friends are sure which ones. What are the possible combinations of 3-D shapes that might create this side profile of the treehouse?

Answer: _____
_____ Marks: ___ /1

③ Miss Dakin is deciding what desserts to make for a party. She wants to make prism-shaped desserts, so that she will be able to slice them into equal portions. There is one dessert below that she should not include. Which one is it? Draw a diagram to explain why this should not be included.

A	B	C	D

She should not include dessert _____, because _____
_____.

Diagram

Marks: ___ /1

Today's Marks: ___ /3

Super Sleuth investigates

In groups of four, debate each of the following motions:

- Triangular prisms are the least useful 3-D shapes.
- Cubes are the most useful 3-D shapes.

Two pupils in the group are for the motion (they agree with it) while the other two are against the motion.

Total Marks: ___ /45 | I can identify and describe 3-D shapes. Yes ☐ No ☐
I can use a Venn diagram to classify shapes. Yes ☐ No ☐

24 Revision 4

Day One Try these.

CLUES

1 In the image above, which two shapes are tessellating in the flag?

Answer: _____ Marks: ___ /2

2 Identify 6 different 2-D shapes in the image above and give one example of where you might see each shape in real life.

Shape	Example in the Image	Example in Real Life

Marks: ___ /6

3 In your copy, the circus management want you to design a new poster to advertise next year's tour, but they are very strict about what they want. You must include an irregular pentagon and an irregular octagon in the design.
You must also draw the name 'Jumbo Circus' using 2-D shapes.

Marks: ___ /1

Puzzle power ✏️

Giggles the Clown loves making gifts for his younger audience members. Today, Giggles is making pentagons and octagons using pipe cleaners. If Giggles has 130 pipe cleaners, how many of each shape can he make, ensuring that there are no pipe cleaners left over? Find all of the possible combinations.

Top tip: Make a table.

Strand: Shape and Space **Strand Units:** 2-D Shapes; Symmetry; 3-D Shapes
Strand: Measures **Strand Unit:** Area

Today's Marks: ___ /9

Day Two Try these.

① Calculate the approximate area of the picture. Estimate first.

CLUES

> **Top tip:**
> Remember that one square represents 1 cm².
> Two half squares add up to 1 cm².
> If greater than half of a square is used,
> it is counted as 1 cm².
> If less than half a square is used,
> it is not counted.

Estimate:

Answer: | **Marks:** /1

② Colour the picture above using four different colours. Measure the area taken up by each colour and record your measurements in the table.

Marks: /4

Colour	Estimate	Area
	cm²	cm²
	cm²	cm²
	cm²	cm²
	cm²	cm²

③ Use the matrix below to help you work out which dressing room each clown uses. Tick the answers.

- Harley does not have the smallest dressing room.
- JoJo's dressing room is 1 m² less in area than Doink's.
- Doink uses the dressing room with the greatest area.
- The area of Harley's dressing room is 2 m² greater than Giggles's.

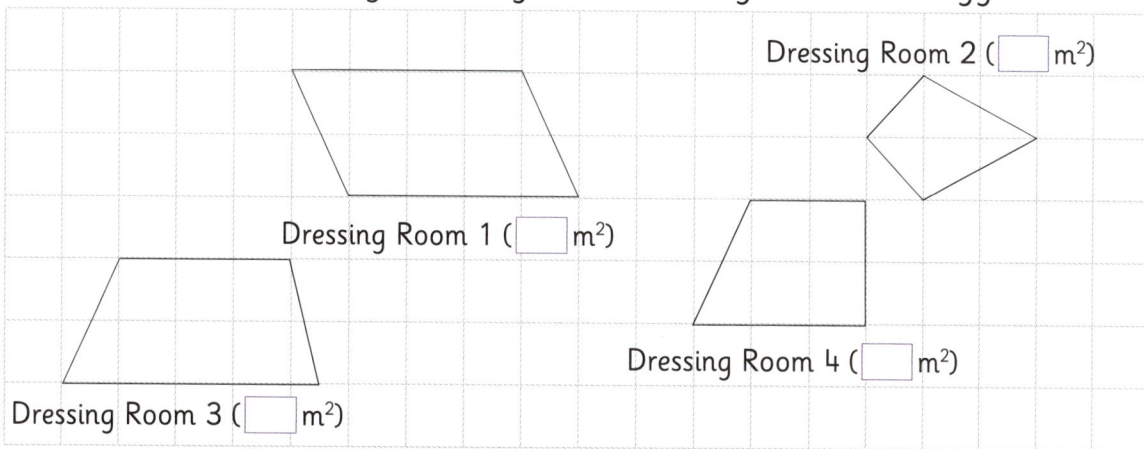

Dressing Room 1 ([ ] m²)

Dressing Room 2 ([ ] m²)

Dressing Room 4 ([ ] m²)

Dressing Room 3 ([ ] m²)

	Room 1	Room 2	Room 3	Room 4
Doink				
Harley				
Giggles				
JoJo				

Marks: /4

Today's Marks: /9

Day Three — Try these.

Complete the following pictures, ensuring that they are symmetrical in both shape and colour.

1

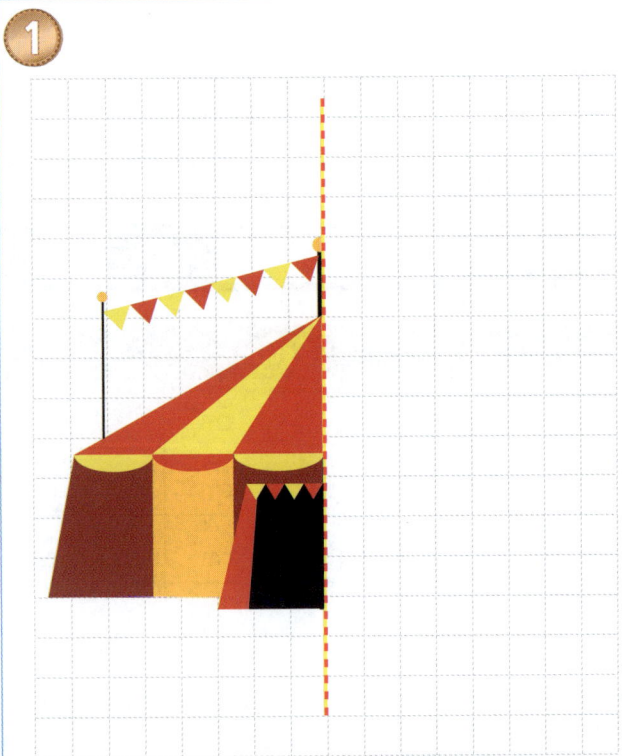

Marks: ☐ /1

2

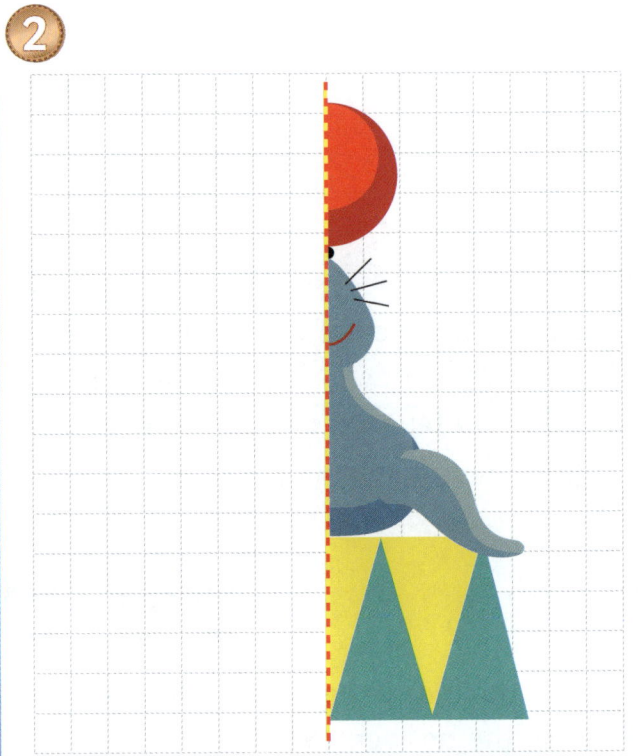

Marks: ☐ /1

3

Marks: ☐ /1

4

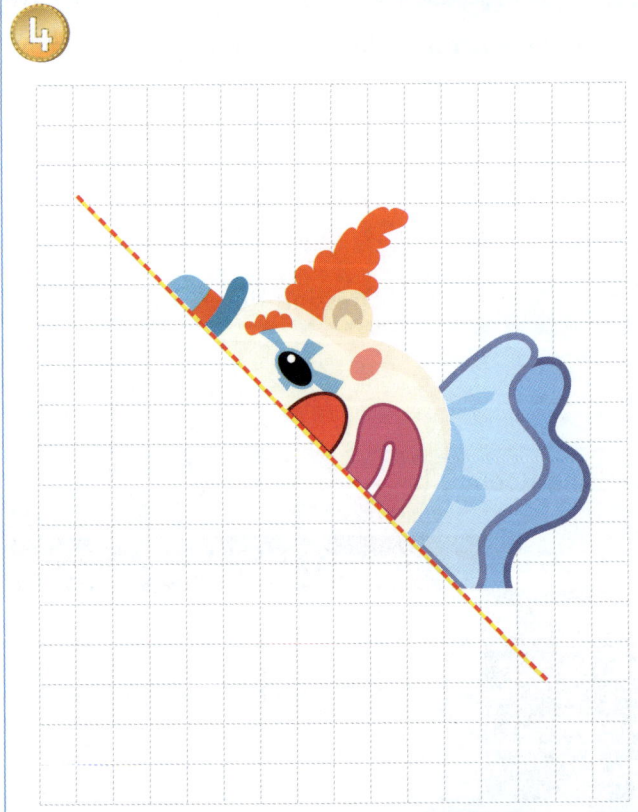

Marks: ☐ /1

Today's Marks: ☐ /4

Day Four Try these.

1 Irina is an aerial artist in the circus and she uses a cube for her performances. Can you label one edge, one face and one vertex on the cube in this image?

Marks: [ ] /3

2 Harry works with the crew that erects the big top when the circus arrives at each location. When he unloaded a truck, he found the 2-D shapes shown in the image. What 3-D shape do you think Harry could make using these shapes? Draw it.

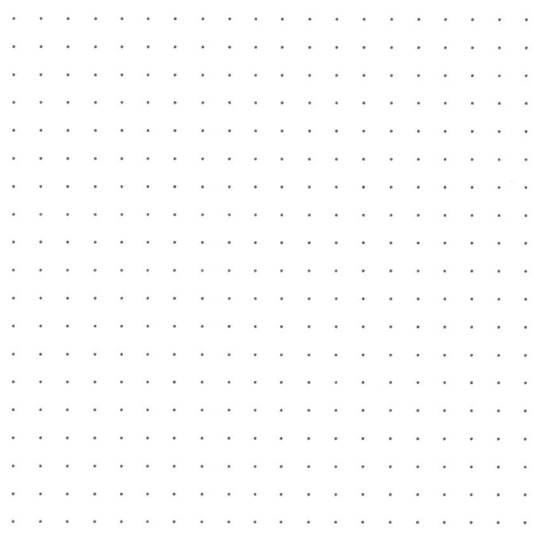

Answer: [ ] Marks: [ ] /2

3 Give one example of a prism that you might see at the circus and where you would expect it to be used.

Answer: [ ] Marks: [ ] /1

4 Many 3-D shapes are made up of 2-D shapes. Think of two examples of 3-D shapes that are not made up of 2-D shapes.

Answer: [ ] Marks: [ ] /2

Today's Marks: [ ] /8

Super Sleuth investigates

Look at the image. You must design a new safety net with an area of 56 m² for this trapeze artist. On a blank piece of paper, draw a rectangle that covers 56 m², using a scale of 1 cm² = 1 m². What measurements (length and width) do you think should be used in the design of the safety net? There are many different possibilities, so make sure that you can justify your decision.

25 Strategy: Act it Out

Day One

The act-it-out strategy involves acting out a situation in a maths story or using concrete materials to break it down, making it easier to solve.

Today, we will use counters and €1 and €2 coins.

One day, David told Mum, "I want to work in a hospital like you, so I don't need to learn about maths." Mum replied, "Let's visit the hospital and I'll show you just how important maths is to the patients, staff and visitors there!"

1. Mum and David met Linda and Martin in the waiting room. How many different ways could all four of them sit together in a row? Use counters to help you or act it out in groups.

Answer: _____ Marks: ___ /1

2. One of the people standing in a queue received a phone call and was overheard saying, "I'm third in line from the receptionist's desk and third from the end of the queue." How many people were in the queue? Use counters to help you or act it out in groups.

Answer: _____ Marks: ___ /1

3. Martin showed David this clever coin puzzle. Can you solve it?

Arrange three €1 coins and three €2 coins like this:	The goal is to end up with the coins arranged like this:
1 2 1 2 1 2	1 1 1 2 2 2

You must place your index and middle fingers on two coins that are side by side and slide them to a new position in the line without rotating them. Only coins that are side by side can be moved to a new position in the line. This puzzle can be solved in three moves!

Answer: _____ Marks: ___ /1

Today's Marks: ___ /3

Day Two Try these.

Today, we will use analogue clock faces and euro and cent coins.

CLUEs

1. Mum and David went to the café for snacks. On the way there, they passed this sign showing the hospital's visiting hours. Calculate how long visitors can spend with patients each day. Use an analogue clock face to help you.

Visitors, please note that visiting hours on the wards are strictly from 2:15 pm to 4:50 pm.

Answer: _____ Marks: ___ /1

2. Mum's friend Rose works in the café. Mum asked Rose how long she was working today. Rose said that she started work at 10:30 am and had taken a 15-minute tea break before noon and a lunch break from 1:15 pm to 2:15 pm. She will take another 15-minute tea break in the afternoon, before finishing work at 5:30 pm. Not including breaks, for how many hours and minutes will Rose work today? Use an analogue clock face to help you.

Answer: _____ Marks: ___ /1

3. Mum gave Rose €7 to pay for the snacks and got back the following coins in change: €1, 50c, 20c and 5c. How much did the snacks cost? Use euro and cent coins to help you.

Answer: _____ Marks: ___ /1

Super Sleuth investigates

Rose received a peculiar order from a customer at the café. He asked for 3 muffins and said that he wanted the 1st muffin to be half the weight of the 2nd muffin. The 3rd muffin, he said, must be the lightest and weigh between 60 g and 100 g. The three muffins must weigh 500 g in total. In groups, use a weighing scales and plasticine to work out the weight of each muffin. You could also use trial and improvement.

For this investigation, you will need a weighing scales and some plasticine.

Today's Marks: ___ /3

Day Three Try these.

Today, we will use counters and analogue clock faces.

CLUES

1 Dr Farrell told Mum and David that over the last 4 days, he had worked 48 hours. If he worked an equal number of hours each day, for how many hours did he work in one day? Use counters to help you.

Answer: _____ Marks: ___ /1

2 Today, Dr Farrell will see each of these patients:

Len	Eithne	Maggie	Josef	Hannah
92 years old	87 years old	43 years old	41 years old	25 years old

- Eithne's appointment is immediately after Hannah's.
- Josef's appointment is before Maggie's.
- The eldest patient has the last appointment.
- Hannah has the third appointment.

Work out the order in which Dr Farrell will see his patients. Use counters to help you or act it out in groups.

1st	2nd	3rd	4th	5th

Marks: ___ /1

3 Dr Farrell will work for only 7 hours and 45 minutes tomorrow, as he has to leave early to go to a parent-teacher meeting. The meeting will start at 3:15 pm and it is a 15-minute drive from the hospital to the school. At what time will he start work? Use an analogue clock face to help you work backwards.

Answer: _____ Marks: ___ /1

Super Sleuth investigates

For this investigation, you will need a measuring jug and water.

A doctor gave a patient a jug containing 1.1 l of water and told him to drink 50 ml per hour. After 9 hours, there was 750 ml of water left in the jug. Did the patient follow the doctor's orders? Act it out.

Today's Marks: ___ /3

Day Four Try these.

Today, we will use counters, analogue clock faces and euro and cent coins.

CLUES

1. At 3:40 pm, Mum went to pay for parking. The screen on the machine was broken, so she had to work out how much she owed. She had arrived at the car park at 2:10 pm. For how long had she been parked? Use an analogue clock face to help you.

Answer: _____ Marks: ___ /1

2. The cost of parking was €2.50 per hour. How much did Mum have to pay for the exact amount of time that her car was parked? Use euro and cent coins to help you.

Answer: _____ Marks: ___ /1

3. The aim of this puzzle is to drive your car out of the car park by moving the other cars out of the way in as few moves as possible. What is the fewest number of moves that you need to make? Use counters to help you.

Answer: _____ Marks: ___ /1

Super Sleuth challenge

Today's Marks: ___ /3

Act out the conversation between David and Mum on the drive home. Was David convinced that maths was an important part of life in a hospital?

Total Marks: ___ /12 | One part of this unit that I found difficult was _____

I will use the act-it-out strategy in the future when _____

26 Number Sentences

We are learning to: Translate an addition, a subtraction, a multiplication or a division number sentence into a maths story. ☐ Translate a one-step maths story into a number sentence. ☐

Day One

Maths stories always contain enough clues for you to solve them. Discuss how you can use the maths language poster below to help you decide which operation to use. What can you do if a maths story does not contain any of these words? 💬

Addition

add	increase
plus	more
and	**+** sum
total	together

Subtraction

take away	remain	take from
minus		fewer
less	**—**	difference
reduce		how many more

Multiplication

multiply	groups of
times	lots of
product	**X** doubled
multiplied by	times tables

Division

divided by	divisible by
share	group
divide	**÷** each
divide into	share equally

Top tip: These questions do not contain words from the maths language poster. Discuss how you can reword them to help you understand what you need to do.

CLUES

Try these.

1. The *Titanic* sank on its maiden voyage in 1912. How many years ago was this?

Answer: _____ Marks: ___ /1

2. If 96 passengers could fit in 6 lifeboats, how many passengers could fit in just one lifeboat?

Answer: _____ Marks: ___ /1

3. The *Titanic* burned 250 kg of coal each hour. How much coal did it burn in one full day (24 hours)?

Answer: _____ Marks: ___ /1

Today's Marks: _____ /3

Day Two Try these.

CLUES

Help Miss Perkins to prepare her maths lesson by changing the number sentences below into word sentences (maths stories). Fill in the missing values first.

1 29 – 11 =

_____

_____ **Marks:** ☐ /2

2 96 + [   ] = 171

_____

_____ **Marks:** ☐ /2

3 42 ÷ [   ] = 6

_____

_____ **Marks:** ☐ /2

4 12 × 8 =

_____

_____ **Marks:** ☐ /2

Puzzle power ✏️ 💬

Number	Number Sentence
12	
20	
10	
8	
9	
15	
48	
27	
16	
36	

Aria's dog has eaten some of the buttons from her calculator! Her friend Alex says that she can use it with just the buttons that are left. Use your calculator to see if this is true. In your copy, try to make the 10 numbers listed on the left using just the buttons that are left on the calculator. You can use each button more than once.

Today's Marks: ☐ /8

109

Day Three Try these.

Sometimes large numbers bamboozle me, so I simplify a puzzle by using smaller numbers. This helps me to work out the method I can use to find the solution.

CLUES

Remember:
> means greater than.
< means less than.

In questions 1 and 2, what is the largest possible whole number that you could use to ensure that the number sentence makes sense?

1 6 + ☐ < 10

Answer: ☐ | Marks: ☐ /1

2 25 + ☐ < 51

Answer: ☐ | Marks: ☐ /1

In questions 3 and 4, what is the smallest possible whole number that you could use to ensure that the number sentence makes sense?

3 16 + ☐ > 30

Answer: ☐ | Marks: ☐ /1

4 57 + ☐ > 194

Answer: ☐ | Marks: ☐ /1

True or false? Write 'T' (true) or 'F' (false) for each of the following number sentences:

(a) $16 - 9 > 7$

(b) $80 = 8 \times 10$

(c) $15 > 4 \times 4$

(d) $11 + 35 < 7 \times 7$

(e) $42 \div 6 > 21 - 14$

(f) $\frac{1}{2}$ of 50 $= \frac{1}{3}$ of 75

Marks: ☐ /6

Today's Marks: ☐ /10

Day Four — Try these.

Super Sleuth challenge

You have 60 seconds to make as many accurate number sentences in your maths copy as you can using the digits and symbols in the table. The winning group is the group with the largest amount of accurate number sentences.

2	50	100	−	5
25	+	15	3	÷
=	30	75	×	20

Duties

Reader
Calculator
Checker
Reporter

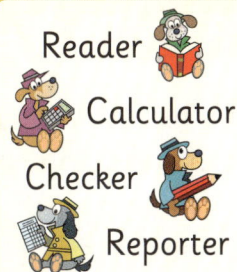

Super Sleuth investigates

Write a number sentence based on the information in each of the pictures below. Use each operation, +, −, ×, ÷, only once.

1. 9 l   54 l

2. €20 €5

3. €58.05

4. €35.90   €29.95

Puzzle power

When you play Scrabble, you are creating number sentences without even realising it! What word can you think of with the greatest value using the Scrabble tiles shown? What would happen if you placed your word on:

- a double word square?
- a triple word square?
- a double letter square?
- a triple letter square?

A_1 B_3 C_3 D_2
E_1 F_4 G_2 H_4 I_1 J_8
K_5 L_1 M_3 N_1 O_1 P_3
Q_{10} R_1 S_1 T_1 U_1 V_4
W_4 X_8 Y_4 Z_{10}

Create puzzles based on this Scrabble board with your partner. Share your puzzles with your classmates.

Total Marks: [ ] /21 | **One part of this unit that I found tricky was** [ ]

Three things that I learned in this unit: [ ]

27 Data

We are learning to: Collect, organise and represent data. ☐ Use pictograms, block graphs, bar charts and bar-line graphs. ☐ Read and interpret bar-line graphs and simple pie charts. ☐

Day One Try these.

CLUES

1 The following pictogram shows the amount of time that Evan spent doing chores last week. Each full picture represents 5 minutes. What was the difference between the time that he spent on the most time-consuming task and the least time-consuming task?

Time Spent on Chores				
Vacuuming	⭐	⭐		
Washing dishes	⭐	⭐	⭐	⯪
Dusting	⭐	⯪		
Hanging out clothes	⭐	⭐	⯪	

Answer: _____ Marks: ☐ /1

2 Look at the pictogram above. How much time did Evan spend doing chores last week?

Answer: _____ Marks: ☐ /1

Super Sleuth investigates 💬

Estimate how long you spent doing the following activities over the weekend:

- Travelling in a car
- Eating food
- Playing games
- Reading

Show this information on a pictogram. What scale will you use? Discuss your pictogram with your partner.

Strand: Data **Strand Unit:** Representing and Interpreting Data

Today's Marks: ☐ /2

Day Two Try these.

Erinsdale National School was awarded a cash prize to spend on technology.
The bar-line graph below shows how the principal decided to spend the winnings.

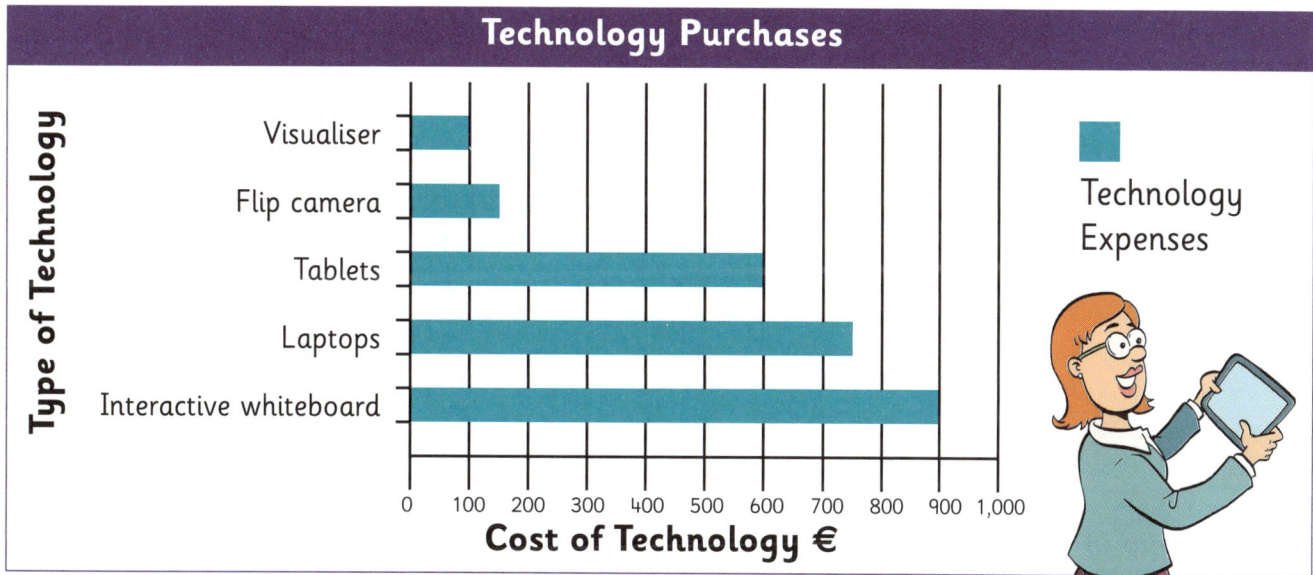

Technology Purchases

Type of Technology

- Visualiser
- Flip camera
- Tablets
- Laptops
- Interactive whiteboard

0 100 200 300 400 500 600 700 800 900 1,000

Cost of Technology €

■ Technology Expenses

1 Which items cost **(a)** the most and **(b)** the least?

Answers: (a)

(b)   Marks: /2

2 If the principal bought 3 laptops, how much did each laptop cost?

Answer: Marks: /1

3 How much more did the principal spend on tablets than on the visualiser and the Flip camera?

Answer: Marks: /1

4 If Erinsdale National School had already owned €6,950 worth of technology, what was the new value of their technology after this win?

Answer: Marks: /1

Today's Marks: /5

Day Three Try these.

1 The pupils in Mr Flynn's class were asked their opinion on homework.

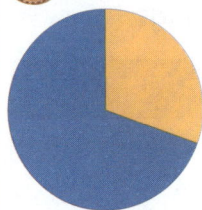

Homework – a good idea or a bad idea?

▢ Good idea
▢ Bad idea

If 18 of the pupils in Mr Flynn's class think that homework is a bad idea, how many think that it is a good idea?

Answer: _____   Marks: ▢ /1

2 A group of teachers were asked what was the best part of their job.

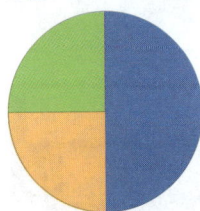

The best thing about being a teacher?

▢ The summer holidays
▢ Working with wonderful children
▢ Giving a lot of homework

If 12 of the teachers chose 'giving a lot of homework', how many teachers said 'working with wonderful children'?

Answer: _____   Marks: ▢ /1

3 How many teachers took part in the survey above altogether?

Answer: _____   Marks: ▢ /1

4 What fraction of the teachers surveyed above chose the summer holidays as the best part of their job?

Answer: _____   Marks: ▢ /1

Today's Marks: ▢ /4

Day Four Try these.

1 As a class, discuss the jobs that you would like to have when you grow up. Each pupil may only choose one job. Select the five most popular jobs and use the tally chart below to record the number of pupils who chose these.

What do you want to be when you grow up?		
Job	**Tally**	**Total**

2 Record the totals from your tally chart on a block graph, a bar chart or a bar-line graph. Use the following checklist to assess your work:

	Pencil and ruler	Title	Accurate scale	Horizontal and vertical axes labelled	Equal space between bars
Marks:	/1	/1	/1	/1	/1

Top tip: You can use the checklist above when drawing all graphs in your maths and science work.

Marks: ☐ /5

Today's Marks: ☐ /5

Total Marks: ☐ /16 | I can use a checklist to correct my graph. | Yes ☐ No ☐

I can answer questions based on different types of graph. | Yes ☐ No ☐

28 Number Patterns and Sequences

We are learning to: Explore, recognise and record patterns in number, 0–9,999. ☐ Describe the rules of sequences in our own words. ☐ Use a hundred square to solve puzzles. ☐

Day One

A number sequence is a list of numbers in a particular order. Sometimes you are told the rule (pattern) for continuing a sequence. On other occasions you must investigate the sequence and work out the rule for yourself. When you see a number sequence for the first time, ask yourself:

- Are the numbers getting bigger or smaller?
- What is the rule?
- What operations will I need to use in order to continue the sequence?

CLUEs

Try these.

Identify the pattern in these number sequences with your partner. You will get one mark for every sequence that you successfully complete and one mark for every rule that you describe accurately.

1. 16, 24, 32, ____ , ____ , ____ .

Rule: _____ Marks: ___ /2

2. 1,120, 1,090, 1,060, ____ , ____ , ____ .

Rule: _____ Marks: ___ /2

3. 7,200, 3,600, 1,800, ____ , ____ , ____ .

Rule: _____ Marks: ___ /2

4. 6, 11, 16, 15, 20, 25, 24, ____ , ____ , ____ .

Rule: _____ Marks: ___ /2

Strand: Algebra **Strand Unit:** Number Patterns and Sequences

Today's Marks: ___ /8

Day Two Try these.

1 Look carefully at the hundred square. Colour the multiples of 4 up to 48. Use the pattern to help you decide if 74 is a multiple of 4 or not.

1	2	3	4	5	6	7	8	9	10
11	12	13	14	15	16	17	18	19	20
21	22	23	24	25	26	27	28	29	30
31	32	33	34	35	36	37	38	39	40
41	42	43	44	45	46	47	48	49	50
51	52	53	54	55	56	57	58	59	60
61	62	63	64	65	66	67	68	69	70
71	72	73	74	75	76	77	78	79	80
81	82	83	84	85	86	87	88	89	90
91	92	93	94	95	96	97	98	99	100

Answer: _____ Marks: [ ] /1

2 Investigate the pattern in the 100 square. Write a rule that describes this pattern.

91	92	93	94	95	96	97	98	99	100
81	82	83	84	85	86	87	88	89	90
71	72	73	74	75	76	77	78	79	80
61	62	63	64	65	66	67	68	69	70
51	52	53	54	55	56	57	58	59	60
41	42	43	44	45	46	47	48	49	50
31	32	33	34	35	36	37	38	39	40
21	22	23	24	25	26	27	28	29	30
11	12	13	14	15	16	17	18	19	20
1	2	3	4	5	6	7	8	9	10

Answer: _____ Marks: [ ] /1

3 The rule is plus 5, minus 1. The last number in the hundred square that this pattern lands on is 98. What is the lowest number that this pattern could have started on? Use the hundred square to help you.

Top tip: Use trial and improvement.

1	2	3	4	5	6	7	8	9	10
11	12	13	14	15	16	17	18	19	20
21	22	23	24	25	26	27	28	29	30
31	32	33	34	35	36	37	38	39	40
41	42	43	44	45	46	47	48	49	50
51	52	53	54	55	56	57	58	59	60
61	62	63	64	65	66	67	68	69	70
71	72	73	74	75	76	77	78	79	80
81	82	83	84	85	86	87	88	89	90
91	92	93	94	95	96	97	98	99	100

Answer: _____ Marks: [ ] /1

4 Write three different number sequences that follow this rule: the number times 4, minus one. (Example: 3, 12, 11, 44, 43, 172.)

(a) _____ , _____ , _____ , _____ , _____ , _____ .

(b) _____ , _____ , _____ , _____ , _____ .

(c) _____ , _____ , _____ , _____ , _____ .

Marks: [ ] /3

Today's Marks: [ ] /6   **117**

Day Three Try these.

1 Mark lives in 1 Henry Street. All of the house numbers on his side of the road are odd. His best friend, Marnie, lives 5 doors down from him on the same side of the road. What is Marnie's house number?

Answer: _____ Marks: ____ /1

2 In January, Ursula began saving for a trip to New York. She saved €15 in January, €20 in February, €25 in March and so on. How much had she saved up in total by the end of December?

Answer: _____ Marks: ____ /1

3 You arrive in Cornmarket Shopping Centre and visit your 1st shop at 3:55 pm. You then visit another shop every 14 minutes. At what time do you arrive at your 4th shop?

Answer: _____ Marks: ____ /1

4 The 1st prize in a competition is €7,500, the 2nd prize is €3,750 and the 3rd prize is €1,875. How much is the 4th prize?

Answer: _____ Marks: ____ /1

Super Sleuth challenge

Danielle won a singing competition and was given two prize options to choose from. Which of the options do you think Danielle should choose if she wants the largest prize, **(a)** or **(b)**?

(a) The value of a 1c coin that has been doubled every day for 20 days

(b) €5,000

Today's Marks: ____ /4

Day Four Try these.

CLUES

1 Complete the number sequences below and colour the squares of the missing values on the hundred square.

(a) 122, 111, 100, ____ , ____ , ____ , ____ , ____ , ____ , ____ , ____ .

(b) 109, 100, 91, ____ , ____ , ____ , ____ , ____ , ____ , ____ , ____ .

1	2	3	4	5	6	7	8	9	10
11	12	13	14	15	16	17	18	19	20
21	22	23	24	25	26	27	28	29	30
31	32	33	34	35	36	37	38	39	40
41	42	43	44	45	46	47	48	49	50
51	52	53	54	55	56	57	58	59	60
61	62	63	64	65	66	67	68	69	70
71	72	73	74	75	76	77	78	79	80
81	82	83	84	85	86	87	88	89	90
91	92	93	94	95	96	97	98	99	100

A letter should now appear on the hundred square!

The letter is ____ .

Marks: ____ /2

2 Create your own hundred square puzzle for your partner.

Marks: ____ /1

3 This diagram shows the first four triangular numbers. What is the 15th triangular number?

1   **3**   **6**   **10**

Answer: _____

Marks: ____ /1

Today's Marks: ____ /4

Total Marks: ____ /22 | **How could you use what you learned in this unit in other topics in maths?**

_____

How could you use what you learned in this unit in other subjects? _____

_____

119

29 Chance

We are learning to: Use the language of chance. ☐
Identify and record outcomes of simple random activities. ☐

Day One

Chance means how likely something is to happen. Another word for this is probability. Here are some chance words that you can use in this unit:

Impossible	The chances of having school on Christmas Day	
Unlikely	The chances of your teacher taking a selfie with you during school	
Possible	The chances that you will have homework on your first day back at school	September 1st Maths – page 1, Q. 1 English – read page 1
Likely	The chances of getting a result that you are proud of if you study for a test	
Certain	The chances that the child sitting next to you is a girl if you attend an all-girls school	

Try these.

1. If you write each letter in the phrase 'Super Sleuth' on separate cards and turn the cards upside down, what are the chances you would pick up the letter 'a' from the set?

Answer: _____ Marks: _ /1

2. If you get caught breaking a serious school rule by your teacher, what are the chances that you will be in trouble?

Answer: _____ Marks: _ /1

3. You think of a number between 1 and 1,000. What is the probability that your teacher will choose your number in one guess?

Answer: _____ Marks: _ /1

4. I have chosen a number between 1 and 6. What are the chances that this number is a factor of 12?

Answer: _____ Marks: _ /1

Today's Marks: ____ /4

Day Two Try these.

Here are some more chance words that you can use to describe the likelihood that something will take place:

Never	A donkey winning a men's 200 m race in the Olympic Games
Even chances	If you roll a dice, there is a 50/50 chance you will roll an even number. Can you explain why this is so?
Definitely	Children in 4th Class are definitely older than 5 years of age.

Write about and draw each of the scenarios below.

1. An example of something that will never happen:

Marks: /1

2. An example of something that has an even chance of happening:

Marks: /1

3. An example of something that will definitely happen:

Marks: /1

4. Super Sleuth overheard a conversation between Edel and Gavin while they were playing darts. Is Edel correct? Explain your answer.

I have no chance of getting a higher score than you, because I have only 1 dart and you have 3!

Marks: /1

Today's Marks: /4   121

Day Three Try these.

1 If you take a T-shirt from this clothesline, what are the chances that it will be red? Explain your answer.

Marks: /1

2 There are 6 slices of cake on a plate: 2 slices of chocolate cake, 2 slices of lemon cake and 2 slices of carrot cake. If you are blindfolded while taking a slice, what is the probability of getting a slice of chocolate cake?

Answer: Marks: /1

3 This spinner is for three players. Each colour on the spinner represents a different player. The aim of the game is to have the spinner land on your colour. If your colour was green, would you be happy with your chances of winning? Explain your answer by comparing your chances with those of red and blue.

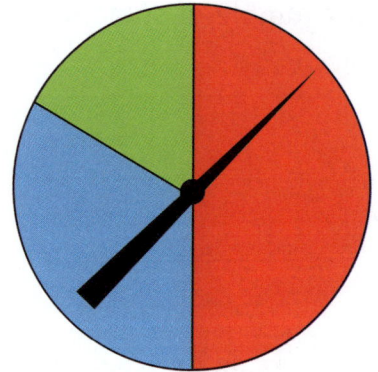

Marks: /1

4 Luke placed 10 cubes in a box: 2 **red**, 3 **orange**, 3 **yellow** and the rest were **green**. If Luke pulled out 4 cubes, which of the following outcomes was impossible?

(a) Luke pulled out 1 **red**, 1 **green** and 2 **orange** cubes.

(b) Luke pulled out 2 **yellow** and 2 **red** cubes.

(c) Luke pulled out 1 **orange** and 3 **green** cubes.

(d) Luke pulled out 4 different colour cubes.

Answer: Marks: /1

Super Sleuth challenge

Make your own spinner for four players, ensuring that everyone will have a fair chance of winning. You must have more than 4 sections in your spinner.

Today's Marks: /4

Day Four Try these.

Winner Takes All! 💬

In pairs, roll a pair of dice. If the sum of the two dice adds up to 2, 3, 4, 10, 11 or 12, player A wins the round. If the sum of the two dice adds up to 5, 6, 7, 8 or 9, player B wins the round. Play ten rounds and keep score.

I predict that player _____ will win this game, because _____

_____

Scoreboard

Roll	1	2	3	4	5	6	7	8	9	10
Player A										
Player B										

Discuss the following with your partner:
- Was your prediction correct?
- Are you surprised by the outcome?
- Which sums were more likely/less likely to be rolled?

You Whinny Some, You Lose Some!

Four horses are taking part in a game show involving a 150 m race. A die is rolled to decide how far each can run.
- Every time a 6 is rolled, Usain Colt runs 50 m.
- Every time an even number is rolled, Neighsayer runs 30 m.
- Every time an odd number is rolled, Sir Trotsalot runs 40 m.
- Every time a 2 or a 5 is rolled, Skedaddle runs 40 m.

1. Who do you think is most likely to cross the finish line first? Why?

2. Who do you think is most likely to cross the finish line last? Why? Act it out using a die!

Duties

Reader
Calculator
Checker
Reporter

Horse	Distance Galloped
Usain Colt	
Neighsayer	
Sir Trotsalot	
Skedaddle	

Total Marks: _____ /12 | Chance words that I used in this unit: _____

The difference between 'definite' and 'likely' is _____

123

30 Revision 5

A Trip to Egypt

Day One **Try these.**

Ciara and her parents are on holidays in Egypt.

1 A tour guide told Ciara and her family that Britain controlled Egypt from 1882 to 1952. For how many years did Britain control Egypt?

Answer: **Marks:** /1

2 On average, it rains for just 12 days a year in Egypt, with 2.5 cm of rainfall each year. In 1980, almost four times this amount of rain fell in one hour in County Antrim. Approximately how much rain fell in Antrim during that hour?

Answer: **Marks:** /1

3 If you add 1 m to the height of the Great Pyramid of Giza and divide the answer by 7, you will get the height of the Great Sphinx. If the Great Sphinx measures 20 m, what is the height of the Great Pyramid of Giza? Work backwards to solve this.

Answer: **Marks:** /1

4 The Ancient Egyptians used hieroglyphs to represent numbers. Decode these hieroglyphic number sentences and find the missing values (regular numbers).

1	10	100	1,000

(a) 𓆼 − | =

(b) 𓆙 ÷ = ∩

(c) 𓆼 + 𓆼 + 𓆙 + ∩ =

(d) 𓆼 − = 𓆙

Marks: /4

Strand: Algebra **Strand Units:** Number Sentences; Number Patterns and Sequences
Strand: Data **Strand Units:** Representing and Interpreting Data; Chance

Today's Marks: /7

Day Two Try these.

The Egyptian tourist board surveyed 100 tourists about their favourite attractions. Here are the results:

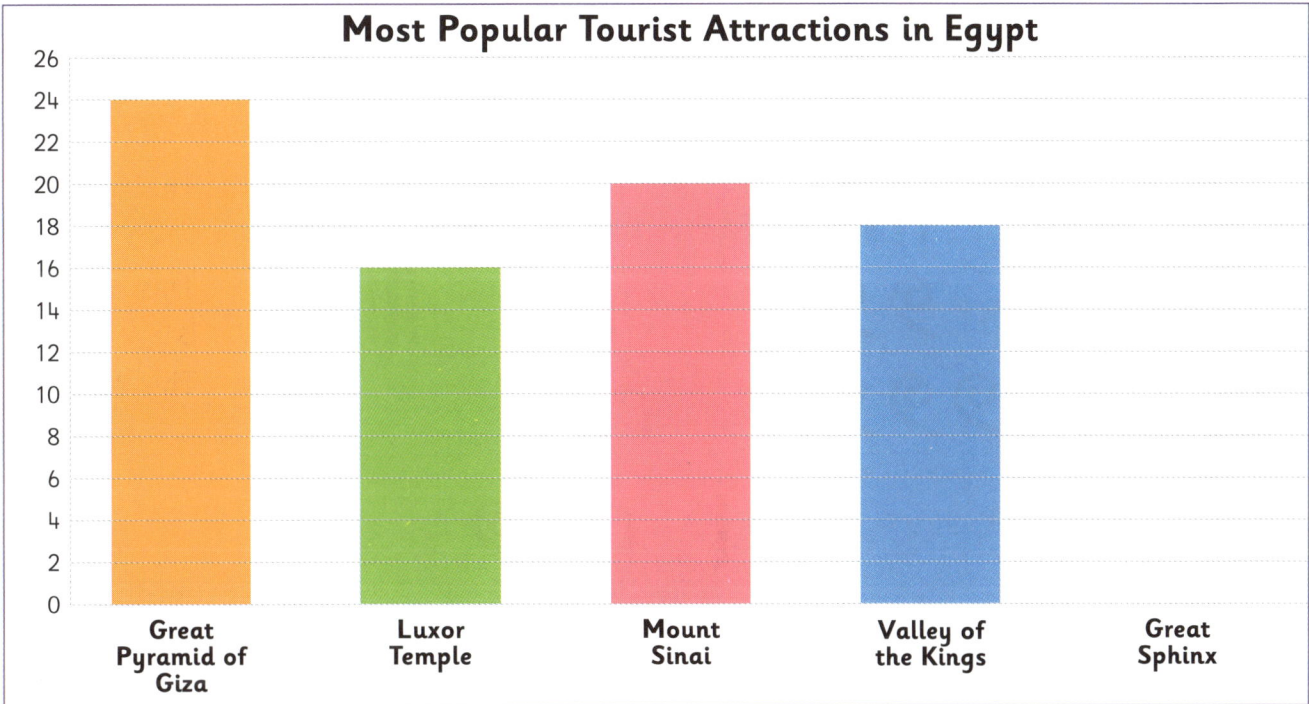

Most Popular Tourist Attractions in Egypt

Bar chart showing number of tourists (y-axis from 0 to 26) for each attraction:
- Great Pyramid of Giza: 24
- Luxor Temple: 16
- Mount Sinai: 20
- Valley of the Kings: 18
- Great Sphinx: (blank)

① Fill in the bar representing the amount of tourists who chose the Great Sphinx as their favourite attraction.

Marks: /1

② What was the least popular tourist attraction among the tourists who were surveyed?

Answer: **Marks:** /1

③ What is the difference between the number of tourists who chose the most popular attraction and the number who chose the least popular attraction?

Answer: **Marks:** /1

④ $\frac{3}{4}$ of the tourists who chose Mount Sinai as their favourite attraction said that they would visit Egypt again. $\frac{4}{9}$ of the tourists who chose Valley of the Kings would also visit Egypt again. How many tourists said that they would visit Egypt again?

Answer: **Marks:** /1

Today's Marks: /4

Day Three Try these.

Ciara and her parents must solve four puzzles to escape a tomb in the Valley of the Kings and they need your help! Change the hieroglyphs to regular numbers. Use number patterns to find the next number in the sequence.

𝐈	∩	𝓰	⚱
1	10	100	1,000

Examples:

∩∩	‖‖‖‖			This number is 24.
⚱⚱	𝓰𝓰	∩	‖‖‖‖‖‖‖‖‖	This number is 2,219.
⚱⚱⚱⚱⚱	𝓰𝓰𝓰𝓰	∩∩	‖‖‖	This number is 5,423.

1 Rule: The number _____.

𝐈	∩	𝓰	

Marks: ☐ /1

2 Rule: The number _____.

∩∩	𝓰	𝓰𝓰𝓰𝓰𝓰	

Marks: ☐ /1

3 Rule: The number _____.

∩∩∩∩∩ ‖‖‖‖‖‖	∩∩∩∩ ‖‖‖‖‖‖‖	∩∩∩∩	

Marks: ☐ /1

4 Rule: The number _____.

𝐈 ∩ 𝐈 ‖‖‖‖‖‖	∩ 𝐈 ‖‖‖‖‖	∩ 𝐈 ‖‖‖	∩∩ 𝐈 ‖‖‖	

Marks: ☐ /1

⚱⚱⚱ 𝓰𝓰𝓰𝓰𝓰𝓰 ∩∩∩∩∩ 𝐈	Total: ☐

When you add all four missing values together, you should get the total shown. Did you help Ciara and her family to escape?

Marks: ☐ /1

Today's Marks: ☐ /5

Day Four   Try these.

1 There are over 700 hieroglyphs in Ancient Egyptian writing. What are the chances that you could guess the one I am thinking of now? Explain your answer.

Marks: ____ /1

2 What are the chances you will visit Egypt some day? Explain your answer.

Marks: ____ /1

3 Ciara has been told that she will fly into the capital city of Egypt. What are the chances she will be landing in an airport in Cairo? Explain your answer.

Marks: ____ /1

4 What are the chances that Ciara will see rain on her trip to Egypt? Use the information given on day one to justify your answer.

Marks: ____ /1

Today's Marks: ____ /4

Super Sleuth challenge

Design two nets to construct cubes. Draw hieroglyph numbers on the six sections of each net. Once you have constructed your two cubes, choose a target number. The aim of the game is to reach your target number in as few rolls as possible.

Player	Roll 1	Roll 2	Roll 3	Roll 4	Roll 5	Roll 6	Roll 7	Roll 8	Target

Duties

Reader

Calculator

Checker

Reporter

Total Marks: ____ /20